The Two Foscari by Lord Byron

AN HISTORICAL TRAGEDY.

George Gordon Byron, 6th Baron Byron, but more commonly known as just Byron was a leading English poet in the Romantic Movement along with Keats and Shelley.

Byron was born on January 22nd, 1788. He was a great traveller across Europe, spending many years in Italy and much time in Greece. With his aristocratic indulgences, flamboyant style along with his debts, and a string of lovers he was the constant talk of society.

In 1823 he joined the Greeks in their war of Independence against the Ottoman Empire, both helping to fund and advise on the war's conduct.

It was an extraordinary adventure, even by his own standards. But, for us, it is his poetry for which he is mainly remembered even though it is difficult to see where he had time to write his works of immense beauty. But write them he did.

He died on April 19th 1824 after having contracted a cold which, on the advice of his doctors, was treated with blood-letting. This cause complications and a violent fever set in. Byron died like his fellow romantics, tragically young and on some foreign field.

"The father softens, but the governor's resolved."—Critic.

I0162224

Index of Contents

INTRODUCTION TO THE TWO FOSCARI
DRAMATIS PERSONÆ
MEN
WOMAN
SCENE - The Ducal Palace, Venice.
ACT I
SCENE I. A Hall in the Ducal Palace.
ACT II
SCENE I. A Hall in the Doge's Palace.
ACT III
SCENE I. The Prison of Jacopo Foscari
ACT IV
SCENE I. A Hall in the Ducal Palace.
ACT V
SCENE I. The Doge's Apartment.
FOOTNOTES:
LORD BYRON – A SHORT BIOGRAPHY
LORD BYRON – A CONCISE BIBLIOGRAPHY

The Two Foscari was produced at Drury Lane Theatre April 7, and again on April 18 and April 25, 1838. Macready played "Frances Foscari," Mr. Anderson "Jacopo Foscari," and Miss Helen Faucit "Marina."

According to the Times, April 9, 1838, "Miss Faucit's Marina, the most energetic part of the whole, was clever, and showed a careful attention to the points which might be made."

Macready notes in his diary, April 7, 1838 (Reminiscences, 1875, ii. 106): "Acted Foscari very well. Was very warmly received ... was called for at the end of the tragedy, and received by the whole house standing up and waving handkerchiefs with great enthusiasm. Dickens, Forster, Procter, Browning, Talfourd, all came into my room."]

INTRODUCTION TO THE TWO FOSCARI

The Two Foscari was begun on June 12, and finished, within the month, on July 9, 1821. Byron was still in the vein of the historic drama, though less concerned with "ancient chroniclers" and original "authorities" (vide ante, Preface to Marino Faliero, vol. iv. p. 332) than heretofore. "The Venetian play," he tells Murray, July 14, 1821, is "rigidly historical;" but he seems to have depended for his facts, not on Sanudo or Navagero, but on Daru's Histoire de la République de Vénise (1821, ii. 520-537), and on Sismondi's Histoire des Républiques ... du Moyen Age (1815, x. 36-46). The story of the Two Doges, so far as it concerns the characters and action of Byron's play, may be briefly re-told. It will be found to differ in some important particulars from the extracts from Daru and Sismondi which Byron printed in his "Appendix to the Two Foscari" (Sardanapalus, etc., 1821, pp. 305-324), and no less from a passage in Smedley's Sketches from Venetian History (1832, ii. 93-105), which was substituted for the French "Pièces justificatives," in the collected edition of 1832-1835, xiii. 198-202, and the octavo edition of 1837, etc., pp. 790, 791.

Francesco, son of Nicolò Foscari, was born in 1373. He was nominated a member of the Council of Ten in 1399, and, after holding various offices of state, elected Doge in 1423. His dukedom, the longest on record, lasted till 1457. He was married, in 1395, to Maria, daughter of Andrea Priuli, and, en secondes noces, to Maria, or Marina, daughter of Bartolommeo Nani. By his two wives he was the father of ten children—five sons and five daughters. Of the five sons, four died of the plague, and the fifth, Jacopo, lived to be the cause, if not the hero, of a tragedy.

The younger of the "Two Foscari" was a man of some cultivation, a collector and student of Greek manuscripts, well-mannered, and of ready wit, a child and lover of Venice, but indifferent to her ideals and regardless of her prejudices and restrictions. He seems to have begun life in a blaze of popularity, the admired of all admirers. His wedding with Lucrezia Contarini (January, 1441) was celebrated with a novel and peculiar splendour. Gorgeous youths, Companions of the Hose (della calza), in jackets of crimson velvet, with slashed sleeves lined with squirrel fur, preceded and followed the bridegroom's train. A hundred bridesmaids accompanied the bride. Her dowry exceeded 16,000 ducats, and her jewels, which included a necklace worn by a Queen of Cyprus, were "rich and rare." And the maiden herself was a pearl of great price. "She behaved," writes her brother, "and does behave, so well beyond what could have been looked for. I believe she is inspired by God!"

Jacopo had everything which fortune could bestow, but he lacked a capacity for right conduct. Four years after his marriage (February 17, 1445) an accusation was laid before the Ten (Romanin, Storia, etc., iv. 266) that, contrary to the law embodied in the Ducal Promissione, he had accepted gifts of jewels and money, not only from his fellow-citizens, but from his country's bitterest enemy, Filippo Visconti, Duke of Milan. Jacopo fled to Trieste, and in his absence the Ten, supported by a giunta of ten, on their own authority and independently of the Doge, sentenced him to perpetual banishment at Nauplia, in Roumania. One of the three Capi di' dieci was Ermolao (or Veneticé Almoro) Donato, of whom more hereafter. It is to be noted that this sentence was never carried into effect. At the end of four months, thanks to the intervention of five members of the Ten, he was removed from Trieste to Treviso, and, two years later (September 13, 1447), out of consideration to the Doge, who pleaded that the exile of his only son prevented him from giving his whole heart and soul to the Republic, permitted to return to Venice. So ends the first chapter of Jacopo's misadventures. He stands charged with unlawful, if not criminal, appropriation of gifts and moneys. He had been punished, but less than he deserved, and, for his father's sake, the sentence of exile had been altogether remitted.

Three years went by, and once again, January, 1451, a charge was preferred against Jacopo Foscari, and on this occasion he was arrested and brought before the Ten. He was accused of being implicated in the murder of Ermolao Donato, who was assassinated November 5, 1450, on leaving the Ducal Palace, where he had been attending the Council of the Pregadi. On the morning after the murder Benedetto Gritti, one of the "avvogadori di Commun," was at Mestre, some five miles from Venice, and, happening to accost a servant of Jacopo's who was loading a barge with wood, asked for the latest news from Venice, and got as answer, "Donato has been murdered!" The possession of the news some hours before it had been made public, and the fact that the newsmonger had been haunting the purlieus of the Ducal Palace on the previous afternoon, enabled the Ten to convict Jacopo. They alleged (Decree of X., March 26, 1451) that other evidence ("testificationes et scripturæ") was in their possession, and they pointed to the prisoner's obstinate silence on the rack—a silence unbroken save by "several incantations and magic words which fell from him," as a confirmation of his guilt. Moreover, it was "for the advantage of the State from many points of view" that convicted and condemned he should be. The question of his innocence or guilt (complicated by the report or tradition that one Nicolò Erizzo confessed on his death-bed that he had assassinated Donato for reasons of his own) is still under discussion. Berlan (I due Foscari, etc., 1852, p. 36) sums up against him. It may, however, be urged in favour of Jacopo that the Ten did not produce or quote the scripturæ et testificationes which convinced them of his guilt; that they stopped short of the death-penalty, and pronounced a sentence inadequate to the crime; and, lastly, that not many years before they had taken into consideration the possibility and advisability of poisoning Filippo Visconti, an event which would, no doubt, have been "to the advantage of the State from many points of view."

Innocent or guilty, he was sentenced to perpetual banishment to the city of Candia, on the north coast of the island of Crete; and, guilty or innocent, Jacopo was not the man to make the best of what remained to him and submit to fate. Intrigue he must, and, five years later (June, 1456), a report reached Venice that papers had been found in his possession, some relating to the Duke of Milan, calculated to excite "nuovi scandali e disordini," and others in cypher, which the Ten could not read. Over and above these papers there was direct evidence that Jacopo had written to the Imperatore dei Turchi, imploring him to send his galley and take him away from Candia. Here was a fresh instance of treachery to the Republic, and, July 21, 1456, Jacopo returned to Venice under the custody of Lorenzo Loredano.

According to Romanin (Storia, etc., iv. 284), he was not put to the torture, but confessed his guilt spontaneously, pleading, by way of excuse, that the letter to the Duke of Milan had been allowed to fall into the hands of spies, with a view to his being recalled to Venice and obtaining a glimpse of his parents and family, even at a risk of a fresh trial. On the other hand, the Dolfin Cronaca, the work of a kinsman of the Foscari, which records Jacopo's fruitless appeal to the sorrowful but inexorable

Doge, and other incidents of a personal nature, testifies, if not to torture on the rack, "to mutilation by thirty strokes of the lash." Be that as it may, he was once more condemned to lifelong exile, with the additional penalty that he should be imprisoned for a year. He sailed for Venice July 31, 1456, and died at Candia, January 12, 1457. Jacopo's misconduct and consequent misfortune overshadowed the splendour of his father's reign, and, in very truth "brought his gray hairs with sorrow to the grave."

After his son's death, the aged Doge, now in his eighty-fifth year, retired to his own apartments, and refused to preside at Councils of State. The Ten, who in 1446 had yielded to the Doge's plea that a father fretting for an exiled son could not discharge his public duties, were instant that he should abdicate the dukedom on the score of decrepitude. Accounts differ as to the mode in which he received the sentence of deposition. It is certain that he was compelled to abdicate on Sunday morning, October 23, 1457, but was allowed a breathing-space of a few days to make his arrangements for quitting the Ducal Palace.

On Monday, October 24, the Great Council met to elect his successor, and sat with closed doors till Sunday, October 30.

On Thursday, October 27, Francesco, heedless of a suggestion that he should avoid the crowd, descended the Giants' Staircase for the last time, and, says the Dolfin Cronaca, "after crossing the courtyard, went out by the door leading to the prisons, and entered his boat by the Ponte di Paglia." "He was dressed," says another chronicle (August. Cod. I, cl. vii.), "in a scarlet mantle, from which the fur lining had been taken," surmounted by a scarlet hood, an old friend which he had worn when his ducal honours were new, and which he had entrusted to his wife's care to be preserved for "red" days and festivals of State. "In his hand he held his staff, as he walked very slowly. His brother Marco was by his side, behind him were cousins and grandsons ... and in this way he went to his own house."

On Sunday, October 30, Pasquale Malipiero was declared Doge, and two days after, All Saints' Day, at the first hour of the morning, Francesco Foscari died. If the interval between ten o'clock on Sunday night and one o'clock on Tuesday morning disproves the legend that the discrowned Doge ruptured a blood-vessel at the moment when the bell was tolling for the election of his successor, the truth remains that, old as he was, he died of a broken heart.

His predecessor, Tomaso Mocenigo, had prophesied on his death-bed that if the Venetians were to make Foscari Doge they would forfeit their "gold and silver, their honour and renown." "From your position of lords," said he, "you will sink to that of vassals and servants to men of arms." The prophecy was fulfilled. "If we look," writes Mr. H. F. Brown (Venice, etc., 1893, p. 306), "at the sum-total of Foscari's reign ... we find that the Republic had increased her land territory by the addition of two great provinces, Bergamo and Brescia ... But the price had been enormous ... her debt rose from 6,000,000 to 13,000,000 ducats. Venetian funds fell to 18-1/2.... Externally there was much pomp and splendour.... But underneath this bravery there lurked the official corruption of the nobles, the suspicion of the Ten, the first signs of bank failures, the increase in the national debt, the fall in the value of the funds. Land wars and landed possessions drew the Venetians from the sea to terra ferma.... The beginning of the end had arrived." (See Two Doges of Venice, by Alethea Wiel, 1891; I due Foscari, Memorie Storicho Critiche, di Francesco Berlan, 1852; Storia Documentata di Venezia, di S. Romanin, 1855, vol. iv.; Die beiden Foscari, von Richard Senger, 1878. For reviews, etc., of The Two Foscari, vide ante, "Introduction to Sardanapalus," p. 5.)

Both Jeffrey in the Edinburgh, and Heber in the Quarterly Review, took exception to the character of Jacopo Foscari, in accordance with the Horatian maxim, "Incredulus odi." "If," said Jeffrey, "he had been presented to the audience wearing out his heart in exile, ... we might have caught some glimpse of the nature of his motives." As it is (in obedience to the "unities") "we first meet with him led from the 'Question,' and afterwards ... clinging to the dungeon walls of his native city, and expiring from his dread of leaving them." The situation lacks conviction.

"If," argued Heber, "there ever existed in nature a case so extraordinary as that of a man who gravely preferred tortures and a dungeon at home, to a temporary residence in a beautiful island and a fine climate; it is what few can be made to believe, and still fewer to sympathize with."

It was, no doubt, with reference to these criticisms that Byron told Medwin (Conversations, 1824, p. 173) that it was no invention of his that the "young Foscari should have a sickly affection for his native city.... I painted the men as I found them, as they were—not as the critics would have them.... But no painting, however highly coloured, can give an idea of the intensity of a Venetian's affection for his native city."

Goethe, on the other hand, was "not careful" to note these inconsistencies and perplexities. He thought that the dramatic handling of The Two Foscari was "worthy of great praise," was "admirable!" (Conversations with Goethe, 1874, p. 265).

DRAMATIS PERSONÆ

MEN
FRANCIS FOSCARI, Doge of Venice.
JACOPO FOSCARI, Son of the Doge.
JAMES LOREDANO, a Patrician.
MARCO MEMMO, a Chief of the Forty.
BARBARIGO, a Senator.

Other Senators, The Council of Ten, Guards, Attendants, etc., etc.

WOMAN
MARINA, Wife of young FOSCARI.

SCENE - The Ducal Palace, Venice.

THE TWO FOSCARI

ACT I

SCENE I. A Hall in the Ducal Palace.

Enter LOREDANO and BARBARIGO, meeting.

LOREDANO - WHERE is the prisoner?

BARBARIGO - Reposing from
The Question.

LOREDANO - The hour's past—fixed yesterday
For the resumption of his trial.—Let us
Rejoin our colleagues in the council, and
Urge his recall.

BARBARIGO - Nay, let him profit by
A few brief minutes for his tortured limbs;
He was o'erwrought by the Question yesterday,
And may die under it if now repeated.

LOREDANO - Well?

BARBARIGO - I yield not to you in love of justice,
Or hate of the ambitious Foscari,
Father and son, and all their noxious race;
But the poor wretch has suffered beyond Nature's
Most stoical endurance.

LOREDANO - Without owning
His crime?

BARBARIGO - Perhaps without committing any.
But he avowed the letter to the Duke
Of Milan, and his sufferings half atone for
Such weakness.

LOREDANO - We shall see.

BARBARIGO - You, Loredano,
Pursue hereditary hate too far.

LOREDANO - How far?

BARBARIGO - To extermination.

LOREDANO - When they are
Extinct, you may say this.—Let's in to council.

BARBARIGO - Yet pause—the number of our colleagues is not
Complete yet; two are wanting ere we can
Proceed.

LOREDANO - And the chief judge, the Doge?

BARBARIGO - No—he,
With more than Roman fortitude, is ever

First at the board in this unhappy process
Against his last and only son.

LOREDANO - True—true—
His last.

BARBARIGO - Will nothing move you?

LOREDANO - Feels he, think you?

BARBARIGO - He shows it not.

LOREDANO - I have marked that—the wretch!

BARBARIGO - But yesterday, I hear, on his return
To the ducal chambers, as he passed the threshold
The old man fainted.

LOREDANO - It begins to work, then.

BARBARIGO - The work is half your own.

LOREDANO - And should be all mine—
My father and my uncle are no more.

BARBARIGO - I have read their epitaph, which says they died
By poison.

LOREDANO - When the Doge declared that he
Should never deem himself a sovereign till
The death of Peter Loredano, both
The brothers sickened shortly:—he is Sovereign.

BARBARIGO - A wretched one.

LOREDANO - What should they be who make
Orphans?

BARBARIGO - But did the Doge make you so?

LOREDANO - Yes.

BARBARIGO - What solid proofs?

LOREDANO - When Princes set themselves
To work in secret, proofs and process are
Alike made difficult; but I have such
Of the first, as shall make the second needless.

BARBARIGO - But you will move by law?

LOREDANO - By all the laws
Which he would leave us.

BARBARIGO - They are such in this
Our state as render retribution easier
Than 'mongst remoter nations. Is it true
That you have written in your books of commerce,
(The wealthy practice of our highest nobles)
"Doge Foscari, my debtor for the deaths
Of Marco and Pietro Loredano,
My sire and uncle?"

LOREDANO - It is written thus.

BARBARIGO - And will you leave it unerased?

LOREDANO - Till balanced.

BARBARIGO - And how?

[Two SENATORS pass over the stage, as in their way to "the Hall of the Council of Ten."

LOREDANO - You see the number is complete.
Follow me.

[Exit LOREDANO.

BARBARIGO - (solus). Follow thee! I have followed long
Thy path of desolation, as the wave
Sweeps after that before it, alike whelming
The wreck that creaks to the wild winds, and wretch
Who shrieks within its riven ribs, as gush
The waters through them; but this son and sire
Might move the elements to pause, and yet
Must I on hardily like them—Oh! would
I could as blindly and remorselessly!—
Lo, where he comes!—Be still, my heart! they are
Thy foes, must be thy victims: wilt thou beat
For those who almost broke thee?

Enter GUARDS, with young JACOPO FOSCARI as Prisoner, etc.

GUARD - Let him rest.
Signor, take time.

JACOPO FOSCARI - I thank thee, friend, I'm feeble;
But thou mayst stand reproved.

GUARD - I'll stand the hazard.

JACOPO FOSCARI - That's kind:—I meet some pity, but no mercy;

This is the first.

GUARD - And might be the last, did they
Who rule behold us.

BARBARIGO - (advancing to the Guard). There is one who does:
Yet fear not; I will neither be thy judge
Nor thy accuser; though the hour is past,
Wait their last summons—I am of "the Ten,"
And waiting for that summons, sanction you
Even by my presence: when the last call sounds,
We'll in together.—Look well to the prisoner!

JACOPO FOSCARI - What voice is that?—'Tis Barbarigo's! Ah!
Our House's foe, and one of my few judges.

BARBARIGO - To balance such a foe, if such there be,
Thy father sits amongst thy judges.

JACOPO FOSCARI - True,
He judges.

BARBARIGO - Then deem not the laws too harsh
Which yield so much indulgence to a sire,
As to allow his voice in such high matter
As the state's safety—

JACOPO FOSCARI - And his son's. I'm faint;
Let me approach, I pray you, for a breath
Of air, yon window which o'erlooks the waters.

Enter an OFFICER, who whispers BARBARIGO.

BARBARIGO - (to the GUARD). Let him approach. I must not speak with him
Further than thus: I have transgressed my duty
In this brief parley, and must now redeem it
Within the Council Chamber.

[Exit BARBARIGO.

[GUARD conducting JACOPO FOSCARI to the window.

GUARD - There, sir, 'tis
Open.—How feel you?

JACOPO FOSCARI - Like a boy—Oh Venice!

GUARD - And your limbs?

JACOPO FOSCARI - Limbs! how often have they borne me
Bounding o'er yon blue tide, as I have skimmed

The gondola along in childish race,
And, masqued as a young gondolier, amidst
My gay competitors, noble as I,
Raced for our pleasure, in the pride of strength;
While the fair populace of crowding beauties,
Plebeian as patrician, cheered us on
With dazzling smiles, and wishes audible,
And waving kerchiefs, and applauding hands,
Even to the goal!—How many a time have I
Cloven with arm still lustier, breast more daring,
The wave all roughened; with a swimmer's stroke
Flinging the billows back from my drenched hair,
And laughing from my lip the audacious brine,
Which kissed it like a wine-cup, rising o'er
The waves as they arose, and prouder still
The loftier they uplifted me; and oft,
In wantonness of spirit, plunging down
Into their green and glassy gulfs, and making
My way to shells and sea-weed, all unseen
By those above, till they waxed fearful; then
Returning with my grasp full of such tokens
As showed that I had searched the deep: exulting,
With a far-dashing stroke, and, drawing deep
The long-suspended breath, again I spurned
The foam which broke around me, and pursued
My track like a sea-bird.—I was a boy then.

GUARD - Be a man now: there never was more need
Of manhood's strength.

JACOPO FOSCARI - (looking from the lattice). My beautiful, my own,
My only Venice—this is breath! Thy breeze,
Thine Adrian sea-breeze, how it fans my face!
Thy very winds feel native to my veins,
And cool them into calmness! How unlike
The hot gales of the horrid Cyclades,
Which howled about my Candiote dungeon, and
Made my heart sick.

GUARD - I see the colour comes
Back to your cheek: Heaven send you strength to bear
What more may be imposed!—I dread to think on't.

JACOPO FOSCARI - They will not banish me again?—No—no,
Let them wring on; I am strong yet.

GUARD - Confess,
And the rack will be spared you.

JACOPO FOSCARI - I confessed
Once—twice before: both times they exiled me.

GUARD - And the third time will slay you.

JACOPO FOSCARI - Let them do so,
So I be buried in my birth-place: better
Be ashes here than aught that lives elsewhere.

GUARD - And can you so much love the soil which hates you?

JACOPO FOSCARI - The soil!—Oh no, it is the seed of the soil
Which persecutes me: but my native earth
Will take me as a mother to her arms.
I ask no more than a Venetian grave,
A dungeon, what they will, so it be here.

Enter an OFFICER.

OFFICER - Bring in the prisoner!

GUARD - Signor, you hear the order.

JACOPO FOSCARI - Aye, I am used to such a summons; 'tis
The third time they have tortured me:—then lend me
Thine arm.   [To the GUARD.

OFFICER - Take mine, sir; 'tis my duty to
Be nearest to your person.

JACOPO FOSCARI - You!—you are he
Who yesterday presided o'er my pangs—
Away!—I'll walk alone.

OFFICER - As you please, Signor;
The sentence was not of my signing, but
I dared not disobey the Council when
They—

JACOPO FOSCARI - Bade thee stretch me on their horrid engine.
I pray thee touch me not—that is, just now;
The time will come they will renew that order,
But keep off from me till 'tis issued. As
I look upon thy hands my curdling limbs
Quiver with the anticipated wrenching,
And the cold drops strain through my brow, as if—
But onward—I have borne it—I can bear it.—
How looks my father?

OFFICER - With his wonted aspect.

JACOPO FOSCARI - So does the earth, and sky, the blue of Ocean,
The brightness of our city, and her domes,

The mirth of her Piazza—even now
Its merry hum of nations pierces here,
Even here, into these chambers of the unknown
Who govern, and the unknown and the unnumbered
Judged and destroyed in silence,—all things wear
The self-same aspect, to my very sire!
Nothing can sympathise with Foscari,
Not even a Foscari.—Sir, I attend you.

[Exeunt JACOPO FOSCARI, OFFICER, etc.

Enter MEMMO and another SENATOR.

MEMMO - He's gone—we are too late:—think you "the Ten"
Will sit for any length of time to-day?

SENATOR - They say the prisoner is most obdurate,
Persisting in his first avowal; but
More I know not.

MEMMO - And that is much; the secrets
Of yon terrific chamber are as hidden
From us, the premier nobles of the state,
As from the people.

SENATOR - Save the wonted rumours,
Which—like the tales of spectres, that are rife
Near ruined buildings—never have been proved,
Nor wholly disbelieved: men know as little
Of the state's real acts as of the grave's
Unfathomed mysteries.

MEMMO - But with length of time
We gain a step in knowledge, and I look
Forward to be one day of the decemvirs.

SENATOR - Or Doge?

MEMMO - Why, no; not if I can avoid it.

SENATOR - 'Tis the first station of the state, and may
Be lawfully desired, and lawfully
Attained by noble aspirants.

MEMMO - To such
I leave it; though born noble, my ambition
Is limited: I'd rather be an unit
Of an united and Imperial "Ten,"
Than shine a lonely, though a gilded cipher.—
Whom have we here? the wife of Foscari?

Enter MARINA, with a female Attendant.

MARINA - What, no one?—I am wrong, there still are two;
But they are senators.

MEMMO - Most noble lady,
Command us.

MARINA - I command!—Alas! my life
Has been one long entreaty, and a vain one.

MEMMO - I understand thee, but I must not answer.

MARINA - (fiercely). True—none dare answer here save on the rack,
Or question save those—

MEMMO - (interrupting her). High-born dame! bethink thee
Where thou now art.

MARINA - Where I now am!—It was
My husband's father's palace.

MEMMO - The Duke's palace.

MARINA - And his son's prison!—True, I have not forgot it;
And, if there were no other nearer, bitterer
Remembrances, would thank the illustrious Memmo
For pointing out the pleasures of the place.

MEMMO - Be calm!

MARINA - (looking up towards heaven). I am; but oh, thou eternal God!
Canst thou continue so, with such a world?

MEMMO - Thy husband yet may be absolved.

MARINA - He is,
In Heaven. I pray you, Signer Senator,
Speak not of that; you are a man of office,
So is the Doge; he has a son at stake
Now, at this moment, and I have a husband,
Or had; they are there within, or were at least
An hour since, face to face, as judge and culprit:
Will he condemn him?

MEMMO - I trust not.

MARINA - But if
He does not, there are those will sentence both.

MEMMO - They can.

MARINA - And with them power and will are one
In wickedness;—my husband's lost!

MEMMO - Not so;
Justice is judge in Venice.

MARINA - If it were so,
There now would be no Venice. But let it
Live on, so the good die not, till the hour
Of Nature's summons; but "the Ten's" is quicker,
And we must wait on't. Ah! a voice of wail!

[A faint cry within.

SENATOR - Hark!

MEMMO - 'Twas a cry of—

MARINA - No, no; not my husband's—
Not Foscari's.

MEMMO - The voice was—

MARINA - Not his: no.
He shriek! No; that should be his father's part,
Not his—not his—he'll die in silence.

[A faint groan again within.

MEMMO - What!
Again?

MARINA - His voice! it seemed so: I will not
Believe it. Should he shrink, I cannot cease
To love; but—no—no—no—it must have been
A fearful pang, which wrung a groan from him.

SENATOR - And, feeling for thy husband's wrongs, wouldst thou
Have him bear more than mortal pain in silence?

MARINA - We all must bear our tortures. I have not
Left barren the great house of Foscari,
Though they sweep both the Doge and son from life;
I have endured as much in giving life
To those who will succeed them, as they can
In leaving it: but mine were joyful pangs:
And yet they wrung me till I could have shrieked,
But did not; for my hope was to bring forth
Heroes, and would not welcome them with tears.

MEMMO - All's silent now.

MARINA - Perhaps all's over; but
I will not deem it: he hath nerved himself,
And now defies them.

Enter an OFFICER hastily.

MEMMO - How now, friend, what seek you?

OFFICER - A leech. The prisoner has fainted.

[Exit OFFICER.

MEMMO - Lady,
'Twere better to retire.

SENATOR - (offering to assist her), I pray thee do so.

MARINA - Off! I will tend him.

MEMMO - You! Remember, lady!
Ingress is given to none within those chambers
Except "the Ten," and their familiars.

MARINA - Well,
I know that none who enter there return
As they have entered—many never; but
They shall not balk my entrance.

MEMMO - Alas! this
Is but to expose yourself to harsh repulse,
And worse suspense.

MARINA - Who shall oppose me?

MEMMO - They
Whose duty 'tis to do so.

MARINA - 'Tis their duty
To trample on all human feelings, all
Ties which bind man to man, to emulate
The fiends who will one day requite them in
Variety of torturing! Yet I'll pass.

MEMMO - It is impossible.

MARINA - That shall be tried.
Despair defies even despotism: there is
That in my heart would make its way through hosts
With levelled spears; and think you a few jailors

Shall put me from my path? Give me, then, way;
This is the Doge's palace; I am wife
Of the Duke's son, the innocent Duke's son,
And they shall hear this!

MEMMO - It will only serve
More to exasperate his judges.

MARINA - What
Are judges who give way to anger? they
Who do so are assassins. Give me way.

[Exit MARINA.

SENATOR - Poor lady!

MEMMO - 'Tis mere desperation: she
Will not be admitted o'er the threshold.

SENATOR - And
Even if she be so, cannot save her husband.
But, see, the officer returns.

[The OFFICER passes over the stage with another person.

MEMMO - I hardly
Thought that "the Ten" had even this touch of pity,
Or would permit assistance to this sufferer.

SENATOR - Pity! Is't pity to recall to feeling
The wretch too happy to escape to Death
By the compassionate trance, poor Nature's last
Resource against the tyranny of pain?

MEMMO - I marvel they condemn him not at once.

SENATOR - That's not their policy: they'd have him live,
Because he fears not death; and banish him,
Because all earth, except his native land,
To him is one wide prison, and each breath
Of foreign air he draws seems a slow poison,
Consuming but not killing.

MEMMO - Circumstance
Confirms his crimes, but he avows them not.

SENATOR - None, save the Letter, which, he says, was written
Addressed to Milan's duke, in the full knowledge
That it would fall into the Senate's hands,
And thus he should be re-conveyed to Venice.

MEMMO - But as a culprit.

SENATOR - Yes, but to his country;
And that was all he sought,—so he avouches.

MEMMO - The accusation of the bribes was proved.

SENATOR - Not clearly, and the charge of homicide
Has been annulled by the death-bed confession
Of Nicolas Erizzo, who slew the late
Chief of "the Ten."

MEMMO - Then why not clear him?

SENATOR - That
They ought to answer; for it is well known
That Almoro Donato, as I said,
Was slain by Erizzo for private vengeance.

MEMMO - There must be more in this strange process than
The apparent crimes of the accused disclose—
But here come two of "the Ten;" let us retire.

[Exeunt MEMMO and Senator.

Enter LOREDANO and BARBARIGO.

BARBARIGO - (addressing LOREDANO).
That were too much: believe me, 'twas not meet
The trial should go further at this moment.

LOREDANO - And so the Council must break up, and Justice
Pause in her full career, because a woman
Breaks in on our deliberations?

BARBARIGO - No,
That's not the cause; you saw the prisoner's state.

LOREDANO - And had he not recovered?

BARBARIGO - To relapse
Upon the least renewal.

LOREDANO - 'Twas not tried.

BARBARIGO - 'Tis vain to murmur; the majority
In council were against you.

LOREDANO - Thanks to you, sir,
And the old ducal dotard, who combined
The worthy voices which o'er-ruled my own.

BARBARIGO - I am a judge; but must confess that part
Of our stern duty, which prescribes the Question,
And bids us sit and see its sharp infliction,
Makes me wish—

LOREDANO - What?

BARBARIGO - That you would sometimes feel,
As I do always.

LOREDANO - Go to, you're a child,
Infirm of feeling as of purpose, blown
About by every breath, shook by a sigh,
And melted by a tear—a precious judge
For Venice! and a worthy statesman to
Be partner in my policy.

BARBARIGO - He shed
No tears.

LOREDANO - He cried out twice.

BARBARIGO - A Saint had done so,
Even with the crown of Glory in his eye,
At such inhuman artifice of pain
As was forced on him; but he did not cry
For pity; not a word nor groan escaped him,
And those two shrieks were not in supplication,
But wrung from pangs, and followed by no prayers.

LOREDANO - He muttered many times between his teeth,
But inarticulately.

BARBARIGO - That I heard not:
You stood more near him.

LOREDANO - I did so.

BARBARIGO - Methought,
To my surprise too, you were touched with mercy,
And were the first to call out for assistance
When he was failing.

LOREDANO - I believed that swoon
His last.

BARBARIGO - And have I not oft heard thee name
His and his father's death your nearest wish?

LOREDANO - If he dies innocent, that is to say,

With his guilt unavowed, he'll be lamented.

BARBARIGO - What, wouldst thou slay his memory?

LOREDANO - Wouldst thou have
His state descend to his children, as it must,
If he die unattainted?

BARBARIGO - War with them too?

LOREDANO - With all their house, till theirs or mine are nothing.

BARBARIGO - And the deep agony of his pale wife,
And the repressed convulsion of the high
And princely brow of his old father, which
Broke forth in a slight shuddering, though rarely,
Or in some clammy drops, soon wiped away
In stern serenity; these moved you not?

[Exit LOREDANO.

He's silent in his hate, as Foscari
Was in his suffering; and the poor wretch moved me
More by his silence than a thousand outcries
Could have effected. 'Twas a dreadful sight
When his distracted wife broke through into
The hall of our tribunal, and beheld
What we could scarcely look upon, long used
To such sights. I must think no more of this,
Lest I forget in this compassion for
Our foes, their former injuries, and lose
The hold of vengeance Loredano plans
For him and me; but mine would be content
With lesser retribution than he thirsts for,
And I would mitigate his deeper hatred
To milder thoughts; but, for the present, Foscari
Has a short hourly respite, granted at
The instance of the elders of the Council,
Moved doubtless by his wife's appearance in
The hall, and his own sufferings. —Lo! they come:
How feeble and forlorn! I cannot bear
To look on them again in this extremity:
I'll hence, and try to soften Loredano.

[Exit BARBARIGO.

ACT II.

SCENE I. A Hall in the Doge's Palace.

The DOGE and a SENATOR.

SENATOR - Is it your pleasure to sign the report
Now, or postpone it till to-morrow?

DOGE - Now;
I overlooked it yesterday: it wants
Merely the signature. Give me the pen—

[The DOGE sits down and signs the paper.

There, Signor.

SENATOR - (looking at the paper). You have forgot; it is not signed.

DOGE - Not signed? Ah, I perceive my eyes begin
To wax more weak with age. I did not see
That I had dipped the pen without effect.

SENATOR - (dipping the pen into the ink, and placing the paper before the DOGE).
Your hand, too, shakes, my Lord: allow me, thus—

DOGE - 'Tis done, I thank you.

SENATOR - Thus the act confirmed
By you and by "the Ten" gives peace to Venice.

DOGE - 'Tis long since she enjoyed it: may it be
As long ere she resume her arms!

SENATOR - 'Tis almost
Thirty-four years of nearly ceaseless warfare
With the Turk, or the powers of Italy;
The state had need of some repose.

DOGE - No doubt:
I found her Queen of Ocean, and I leave her
Lady of Lombardy; it is a comfort
That I have added to her diadem
The gems of Brescia and Ravenna; Crema
And Bergamo no less are hers; her realm
By land has grown by thus much in my reign,
While her sea-sway has not shrunk.

SENATOR - 'Tis most true,
And merits all our country's gratitude.

DOGE - Perhaps so.

SENATOR - Which should be made manifest.

DOGE - I have not complained, sir.

SENATOR - My good Lord, forgive me.

DOGE - For what?

SENATOR - My heart bleeds for you.

DOGE - For me, Signor?

SENATOR - And for your—

DOGE - Stop!

SENATOR - It must have way, my Lord:
I have too many duties towards you
And all your house, for past and present kindness,
Not to feel deeply for your son.

DOGE - Was this
In your commission?

SENATOR - What, my Lord?

DOGE - This prattle
Of things you know not: but the treaty's signed;
Return with it to them who sent you.

SENATOR - I
Obey. I had in charge, too, from the Council,
That you would fix an hour for their reunion.

DOGE - Say, when they will—now, even at this moment,
If it so please them: I am the State's servant.

SENATOR - They would accord some time for your repose.

DOGE - I have no repose, that is, none which shall cause
The loss of an hour's time unto the State.
Let them meet when they will, I shall be found
Where I should be, and what I have been ever.

[Exit SENATOR. The DOGE remains in silence.

Enter an ATTENDANT.

ATTENDANT - Prince!

DOGE - Say on.

ATTENDANT - The illustrious lady Foscari
Requests an audience.

DOGE - Bid her enter. Poor
Marina!

[Exit ATTENDANT. The DOGE remains in silence as before.

Enter MARINA.

MARINA - I have ventured, father, on
Your privacy.

DOGE - I have none from you, my child.
Command my time, when not commanded by
The State.

MARINA - I wished to speak to you of him.

DOGE - Your husband?

MARINA - And your son.

DOGE - Proceed, my daughter!

MARINA - I had obtained permission from "the Ten"
To attend my husband for a limited number
Of hours.

DOGE - You had so.

MARINA - 'Tis revoked.

DOGE - By whom?

MARINA - "The Ten."—When we had reached "the Bridge of Sighs,"
Which I prepared to pass with Foscari,
The gloomy guardian of that passage first
Demurred: a messenger was sent back to
"The Ten;"—but as the Court no longer sate,
And no permission had been given in writing,
I was thrust back, with the assurance that
Until that high tribunal reassembled
The dungeon walls must still divide us.

DOGE - True,
The form has been omitted in the haste
With which the court adjourned; and till it meets,
'Tis dubious.

MARINA - Till it meets! and when it meets,
They'll torture him again; and he and I
Must purchase by renewal of the rack
The interview of husband and of wife,
The holiest tie beneath the Heavens!—Oh God!
Dost thou see this?

DOGE - Child—child—

MARINA - (abruptly) Call me not "child!"
You soon will have no children—you deserve none—
You, who can talk thus calmly of a son
In circumstances which would call forth tears
Of blood from Spartans! Though these did not weep
Their boys who died in battle, is it written
That they beheld them perish piecemeal, nor
Stretched forth a hand to save them?

DOGE - You behold me:
I cannot weep—I would I could; but if
Each white hair on this head were a young life,
This ducal cap the Diadem of earth,
This ducal ring with which I wed the waves
A talisman to still them—I'd give all
For him.

MARINA - With less he surely might be saved.

DOGE - That answer only shows you know not Venice.
Alas! how should you? she knows not herself,
In all her mystery. Hear me—they who aim
At Foscari, aim no less at his father;
The sire's destruction would not save the son;
They work by different means to the same end,
And that is—but they have not conquered yet.

MARINA - But they have crushed.

DOGE - Nor crushed as yet—I live.

MARINA - And your son,—how long will he live?

DOGE - I trust,
For all that yet is past, as many years
And happier than his father. The rash boy,
With womanish impatience to return,
Hath ruined all by that detected letter:
A high crime, which I neither can deny
Nor palliate, as parent or as Duke:
Had he but borne a little, little longer
His Candiote exile, I had hopes—he has quenched them—

He must return.

MARINA - To exile?

DOGE - I have said it.

MARINA - And can I not go with him?

DOGE - You well know
This prayer of yours was twice denied before
By the assembled "Ten," and hardly now
Will be accorded to a third request,
Since aggravated errors on the part
Of your Lord renders them still more austere.

MARINA - Austere? Atrocious! The old human fiends,
With one foot in the grave, with dim eyes, strange
To tears save drops of dotage, with long white
And scanty hairs, and shaking hands, and heads
As palsied as their hearts are hard, they counsel,
Cabal, and put men's lives out, as if Life
Were no more than the feelings long extinguished
In their acccurséd bosoms.

DOGE - You know not—

MARINA - I do—I do—and so should you, methinks—
That these are demons: could it be else that
Men, who have been of women born and suckled—
Who have loved, or talked at least of Love—have given
Their hands in sacred vows—have danced their babes
Upon their knees, perhaps have mourned above them—
In pain, in peril, or in death—who are,
Or were, at least in seeming, human, could
Do as they have done by yours, and you yourself—
You, who abet them?

DOGE - I forgive this, for
You know not what you say.

MARINA - You know it well,
And feel it nothing.

DOGE - I have borne so much,
That words have ceased to shake me.

MARINA - Oh, no doubt!
You have seen your son's blood flow, and your flesh shook not;
And after that, what are a woman's words?
No more than woman's tears, that they should shake you.

DOGE - Woman, this clamorous grief of thine, I tell thee,
Is no more in the balance weighed with that
Which—but I pity thee, my poor Marina!

MARINA - Pity my husband, or I cast it from me;
Pity thy son! Thou pity!—'tis a word
Strange to thy heart—how came it on thy lips?

DOGE - I must bear these reproaches, though they wrong me.
Couldst thou but read—

MARINA - 'Tis not upon thy brow,
Nor in thine eyes, nor in thine acts,—where then
Should I behold this sympathy? or shall?

DOGE - (pointing downwards). There.

MARINA - In the earth?

DOGE - To which I am tending: when
It lies upon this heart, far lightlier, though
Loaded with marble, than the thoughts which press it
Now, you will know me better.

MARINA - Are you, then,
Indeed, thus to be pitied?

DOGE - Pitied! None
Shall ever use that base word, with which men
Cloak their soul's hoarded triumph, as a fit one
To mingle with my name; that name shall be,
As far as I have borne it, what it was
When I received it.

MARINA - But for the poor children
Of him thou canst not, or thou wilt not save,
You were the last to bear it.

DOGE - Would it were so!
Better for him he never had been born;
Better for me.—I have seen our house dishonoured.

MARINA - That's false! A truer, nobler, trustier heart,
More loving, or more loyal, never beat
Within a human breast. I would not change
My exiled, persecuted, mangled husband,
Oppressed but not disgraced, crushed, overwhelmed,
Alive, or dead, for Prince or Paladin
In story or in fable, with a world
To back his suit. Dishonoured!—he dishonoured!
I tell thee, Doge, 'tis Venice is dishonoured;

His name shall be her foulest, worst reproach,
For what he suffers, not for what he did.
'Tis ye who are all traitors, Tyrant!—ye!
Did you but love your Country like this victim
Who totters back in chains to tortures, and
Submits to all things rather than to exile,
You'd fling yourselves before him, and implore
His grace for your enormous guilt.

DOGE - He was
Indeed all you have said. I better bore
The deaths of the two sons Heaven took from me,
Than Jacopo's disgrace.

MARINA - That word again?

DOGE - Has he not been condemned?

MARINA - Is none but guilt so?

DOGE - Time may restore his memory—I would hope so.
He was my pride, my—but 'tis useless now—
I am not given to tears, but wept for joy
When he was born: those drops were ominous.

MARINA - I say he's innocent! And were he not so,
Is our own blood and kin to shrink from us
In fatal moments?

DOGE - I shrank not from him:
But I have other duties than a father's;
The state would not dispense me from those duties;
Twice I demanded it, but was refused:
They must then be fulfilled.

Enter an ATTENDANT.

ATTENDANT - A message from
"The Ten."

DOGE - Who bears it?

ATTENDANT - Noble Loredano.

DOGE - He!—but admit him.

[Exit ATTENDANT.

MARINA - Must I then retire?

DOGE - Perhaps it is not requisite, if this

Concerns your husband, and if not—Well, Signor,

[To LOREDANO entering.

Your pleasure?

LOREDANO - I bear that of "the Ten."

DOGE - They
Have chosen well their envoy.

LOREDANO - 'Tis their choice
Which leads me here.

DOGE - It does their wisdom honour,
And no less to their courtesy.—Proceed.

LOREDANO - We have decided.

DOGE - We?

LOREDANO - "The Ten" in council.

DOGE - What! have they met again, and met without
Apprising me?

LOREDANO - They wished to spare your feelings,
No less than age.

DOGE - That's new—when spared they either?
I thank them, notwithstanding.

LOREDANO - You know well
That they have power to act at their discretion,
With or without the presence of the Doge.

DOGE - 'Tis some years since I learned this, long before
I became Doge, or dreamed of such advancement.
You need not school me, Signor; I sate in
That Council when you were a young patrician.

LOREDANO - True, in my father's time; I have heard him and
The Admiral, his brother, say as much.
Your Highness may remember them; they both
Died suddenly.

DOGE - And if they did so, better
So die than live on lingeringly in pain.

LOREDANO - No doubt: yet most men like to live their days out.

DOGE - And did not they?

LOREDANO - The Grave knows best: they died,
As I said, suddenly.

DOGE - Is that so strange,
That you repeat the word emphatically?

LOREDANO - So far from strange, that never was there death
In my mind half so natural as theirs.
Think you not so?

DOGE - What should I think of mortals?

LOREDANO - That they have mortal foes.

DOGE - I understand you;
Your sires were mine, and you are heir in all things.

LOREDANO - You best know if I should be so.

DOGE - I do.
Your fathers were my foes, and I have heard
Foul rumours were abroad; I have also read
Their epitaph, attributing their deaths
To poison. 'Tis perhaps as true as most
Inscriptions upon tombs, and yet no less
A fable.

LOREDANO - Who dares say so?

DOGE - I!—'Tis true
Your fathers were mine enemies, as bitter
As their son e'er can be, and I no less
Was theirs; but I was openly their foe:
I never worked by plot in Council, nor
Cabal in commonwealth, nor secret means
Of practice against life by steel or drug.
The proof is—your existence.

LOREDANO - I fear not.

DOGE - You have no cause, being what I am; but were I
That you would have me thought, you long ere now
Were past the sense of fear. Hate on; I care not.

LOREDANO - I never yet knew that a noble's life
In Venice had to dread a Doge's frown,
That is, by open means.

DOGE - But I, good Signor,

Am, or at least was, more than a mere duke,
In blood, in mind, in means; and that they know
Who dreaded to elect me, and have since
Striven all they dare to weigh me down: be sure,
Before or since that period, had I held you
At so much price as to require your absence,
A word of mine had set such spirits to work
As would have made you nothing. But in all things
I have observed the strictest reverence;
Not for the laws alone, for those you have strained
(I do not speak of you but as a single
Voice of the many) somewhat beyond what
I could enforce for my authority,
Were I disposed to brawl; but, as I said,
I have observed with veneration, like
A priest's for the High Altar, even unto
The sacrifice of my own blood and quiet,
Safety, and all save honour, the decrees,
The health, the pride, and welfare of the State.
And now, sir, to your business.

LOREDANO - 'Tis decreed,
That, without further repetition of
The Question, or continuance of the trial,
Which only tends to show how stubborn guilt is,
("The Ten," dispensing with the stricter law
Which still prescribes the Question till a full
Confession, and the prisoner partly having
Avowed his crime in not denying that
The letter to the Duke of Milan's his),
James Foscari return to banishment,
And sail in the same galley which conveyed him.

MARINA - Thank God! At least they will not drag him more
Before that horrible tribunal. Would he
But think so, to my mind the happiest doom,
Not he alone, but all who dwell here, could
Desire, were to escape from such a land.

DOGE - That is not a Venetian thought, my daughter.

MARINA - No, 'twas too human. May I share his exile?

LOREDANO - Of this "the Ten" said nothing.

MARINA - So I thought!
That were too human, also. But it was not
Inhibited?

LOREDANO - It was not named.

MARINA - (to the DOGE) - Then, father,
Surely you can obtain or grant me thus much:
[To LOREDANO.
And you, sir, not oppose my prayer to be
Permitted to accompany my husband.

DOGE - I will endeavour.

MARINA - And you, Signor?

LOREDANO - Lady!
'Tis not for me to anticipate the pleasure
Of the tribunal.

MARINA - Pleasure! what a word
To use for the decrees of—

DOGE - Daughter, know you
In what a presence you pronounce these things?

MARINA - A Prince's and his subject's.

LOREDANO - Subject!

MARINA - Oh!
It galls you:—well, you are his equal, as
You think; but that you are not, nor would be,
Were he a peasant:—well, then, you're a Prince,
A princely noble; and what then am I?

LOREDANO - The offspring of a noble house.

MARINA - And wedded
To one as noble. What, or whose, then, is
The presence that should silence my free thoughts?

LOREDANO - The presence of your husband's Judges.

DOGE - And
The deference due even to the lightest word
That falls from those who rule in Venice.

MARINA - Keep
Those maxims for your mass of scared mechanics,
Your merchants, your Dalmatian and Greek slaves,
Your tributaries, your dumb citizens,
And masked nobility, your sbirri, and
Your spies, your galley and your other slaves,
To whom your midnight carryings off and drownings,
Your dungeons next the palace roofs, or under
The water's level; your mysterious meetings,

And unknown dooms, and sudden executions,
Your "Bridge of Sighs," your strangling chamber, and
Your torturing instruments, have made ye seem
The beings of another and worse world!
Keep such for them: I fear ye not. I know ye;
Have known and proved your worst, in the infernal
Process of my poor husband! Treat me as
Ye treated him:—you did so, in so dealing
With him. Then what have I to fear from you,
Even if I were of fearful nature, which
I trust I am not?

DOGE - You hear, she speaks wildly.

MARINA - Not wisely, yet not wildly.

LOREDANO - Lady! words
Uttered within these walls I bear no further
Than to the threshold, saving such as pass
Between the Duke and me on the State's service.
Doge! have you aught in answer?

DOGE - Something from
The Doge; it may be also from a parent.

LOREDANO - My mission here is to the DOGE -

DOGE - Then say
The Doge will choose his own ambassador,
Or state in person what is meet; and for
The father—

LOREDANO - I remember mine.—Farewell!
I kiss the hands of the illustrious Lady,
And bow me to the Duke.

[Exit LOREDANO.

MARINA - Are you content?

DOGE - I am what you behold.

MARINA - And that's a mystery.

DOGE - All things are so to mortals; who can read them
Save he who made? or, if they can, the few
And gifted spirits, who have studied long
That loathsome volume—man, and pored upon
Those black and bloody leaves, his heart and brain,
But learn a magic which recoils upon
The adept who pursues it: all the sins

We find in others, Nature made our own;
All our advantages are those of Fortune;
Birth, wealth, health, beauty, are her accidents,
And when we cry out against Fate, 'twere well
We should remember Fortune can take nought
Save what she gave—the rest was nakedness,
And lusts, and appetites, and vanities,
The universal heritage, to battle
With as we may, and least in humblest stations,
Where Hunger swallows all in one low want,
And the original ordinance, that man
Must sweat for his poor pittance, keeps all passions
Aloof, save fear of famine! All is low,
And false, and hollow—clay from first to last,
The Prince's urn no less than potter's vessel.
Our Fame is in men's breath, our lives upon
Less than their breath; our durance upon days
Our days on seasons; our whole being on
Something which is not us!—So, we are slaves,
The greatest as the meanest—nothing rests
Upon our will; the will itself no less
Depends upon a straw than on a storm;
And when we think we lead, we are most led,
And still towards Death, a thing which comes as much
Without our act or choice as birth, so that
Methinks we must have sinned in some old world,
And this is Hell: the best is, that it is not
Eternal.

MARINA - These are things we cannot judge
On earth.

DOGE - And how then shall we judge each other,
Who are all earth, and I, who am called upon
To judge my son? I have administered
My country faithfully—victoriously—
I dare them to the proof, the chart of what
She was and is: my reign has doubled realms;
And, in reward, the gratitude of Venice
Has left, or is about to leave, me single.

MARINA - And Foscari? I do not think of such things,
So I be left with him.

DOGE - You shall be so;
Thus much they cannot well deny.

MARINA - And if
They should, I will fly with him.

DOGE - That can ne'er be.

And whither would you fly?

MARINA - I know not, reck not—
To Syria, Egypt, to the Ottoman—
Any where, where we might respire unfettered,
And live nor girt by spies, nor liable
To edicts of inquisitors of state.

DOGE - What, wouldst thou have a renegade for husband,
And turn him into traitor?

MARINA - He is none!
The Country is the traitress, which thrusts forth
Her best and bravest from her. Tyranny
Is far the worst of treasons. Dost thou deem
None rebels except subjects? The Prince who
Neglects or violates his trust is more
A brigand than the robber-chief.

DOGE - I cannot
Charge me with such a breach of faith.

MARINA - No; thou
Observ'st, obey'st such laws as make old Draco's
A code of mercy by comparison.

DOGE - I found the law; I did not make it. Were I
A subject, still I might find parts and portions
Fit for amendment; but as Prince, I never
Would change, for the sake of my house, the charter
Left by our fathers.

MARINA - Did they make it for
The ruin of their children?

DOGE - Under such laws, Venice
Has risen to what she is—a state to rival
In deeds, and days, and sway, and, let me add,
In glory (for we have had Roman spirits
Amongst us), all that history has bequeathed
Of Rome and Carthage in their best times, when
The people swayed by Senates.

MARINA - Rather say,
Groaned under the stern Oligarchs.

DOGE - Perhaps so;
But yet subdued the World: in such a state
An individual, be he richest of
Such rank as is permitted, or the meanest,
Without a name, is alike nothing, when

The policy, irrevocably tending
To one great end, must be maintained in vigour.

MARINA - This means that you are more a Doge than father.

DOGE - It means, I am more citizen than either.
If we had not for many centuries
Had thousands of such citizens, and shall,
I trust, have still such, Venice were no city.

MARINA - Accurséd be the city where the laws
Would stifle Nature's!

DOGE - Had I as many sons
As I have years, I would have given them all,
Not without feeling, but I would have given them
To the State's service, to fulfil her wishes,
On the flood, in the field, or, if it must be,
As it, alas! has been, to ostracism,
Exile, or chains, or whatsoever worse
She might decree.

MARINA - And this is Patriotism?
To me it seems the worst barbarity.
Let me seek out my husband: the sage "Ten,"
With all its jealousy, will hardly war
So far with a weak woman as deny me
A moment's access to his dungeon.

DOGE - I'll
So far take on myself, as order that
You may be admitted.

MARINA - And what shall I say
To Foscari from his father?

DOGE - That he obey
The laws.

MARINA - And nothing more? Will you not see him
Ere he depart? It may be the last time.

DOGE - The last!—my boy!—the last time I shall see
My last of children! Tell him I will come.

[Exeunt.

ACT III

SCENE I. The Prison of Jacopo Foscari

JACOPO FOSCARI - (solus).
No light, save yon faint gleam which shows me walls
Which never echoed but to Sorrow's sounds,
The sigh of long imprisonment, the step
Of feet on which the iron clanked the groan
Of Death, the imprecation of Despair!
And yet for this I have returned to Venice,
With some faint hope, 'tis true, that Time, which wears
The marble down, had worn away the hate
Of men's hearts; but I knew them not, and here
Must I consume my own, which never beat
For Venice but with such a yearning as
The dove has for her distant nest, when wheeling
High in the air on her return to greet
Her callow brood. What letters are these which

[Approaching the wall.

Are scrawled along the inexorable wall?
Will the gleam let me trace them? Ah! the names
Of my sad predecessors in this place,
The dates of their despair, the brief words of
A grief too great for many. This stone page
Holds like an epitaph their history;
And the poor captive's tale is graven on
His dungeon barrier, like the lover's record
Upon the bark of some tall tree, which bears
His own and his belovéd's name. Alas!
I recognise some names familiar to me,
And blighted like to mine, which I will add,
Fittest for such a chronicle as this,
Which only can be read, as writ, by wretches.

[He engraves his name.

Enter a FAMILIAR of "the Ten."

FAMILIAR - I bring you food.

JACOPO FOSCARI - I pray you set it down;
I am past hunger: but my lips are parched—
The water!

FAMILIAR - There.

JACOPO FOSCARI - (after drinking). I thank you: I am better.

FAMILIAR - I am commanded to inform you that
Your further trial is postponed.

JACOPO FOSCARI - Till when?

FAMILIAR - I know not.—It is also in my orders
That your illustrious lady be admitted.

JACOPO FOSCARI - Ah! they relent, then—I had ceased to hope it:
'Twas time.

Enter MARINA.

MARINA - My best belovéd!

JACOPO FOSCARI - (embracing her). My true wife,
And only friend! What happiness!

MARINA - We'll part
No more.

JACOPO FOSCARI - How! would'st thou share a dungeon?

MARINA - Aye,
The rack, the grave, all—any thing with thee,
But the tomb last of all, for there we shall
Be ignorant of each other, yet I will
Share that—all things except new separation;
It is too much to have survived the first.
How dost thou? How are those worn limbs? Alas!
Why do I ask? Thy paleness—

JACOPO FOSCARI - 'Tis the joy
Of seeing thee again so soon, and so
Without expectancy, has sent the blood
Back to my heart, and left my cheeks like thine,
For thou art pale too, my Marina!

MARINA - 'Tis
The gloom of this eternal cell, which never
Knew sunbeam, and the sallow sullen glare
Of the familiar's torch, which seems akin
To darkness more than light, by lending to
The dungeon vapours its bituminous smoke,
Which cloud whate'er we gaze on, even thine eyes—
No, not thine eyes—they sparkle—how they sparkle!

JACOPO FOSCARI - And thine!—but I am blinded by the torch.

MARINA - As I had been without it. Couldst thou see here?

JACOPO FOSCARI - Nothing at first; but use and time had taught me
Familiarity with what was darkness;

And the grey twilight of such glimmerings as
Glide through the crevices made by the winds
Was kinder to mine eyes than the full Sun,
When gorgeously o'ergilding any towers
Save those of Venice; but a moment ere
Thou earnest hither I was busy writing.

MARINA - What?

JACOPO FOSCARI - My name: look, 'tis there—recorded next
The name of him who here preceded me,—
If dungeon dates say true.

MARINA - And what of him?

JACOPO FOSCARI - These walls are silent of men's ends; they only
Seem to hint shrewdly of them. Such stern walls
Were never piled on high save o'er the dead,
Or those who soon must be so.—What of him?
Thou askest.—What of me? may soon be asked,
With the like answer—doubt and dreadful surmise—
Unless thou tell'st my tale.

MARINA - I speak of thee!

JACOPO FOSCARI - And wherefore not? All then shall speak of me:
The tyranny of silence is not lasting,
And, though events be hidden, just men's groans
Will burst all cerement, even a living grave's!
I do not doubt my memory, but my life;
And neither do I fear.

MARINA - Thy life is safe.

JACOPO FOSCARI - And liberty?

MARINA - The mind should make its own!

JACOPO FOSCARI - That has a noble sound; but 'tis a sound,
A music most impressive, but too transient:
The Mind is much, but is not all. The Mind
Hath nerved me to endure the risk of death,
And torture positive, far worse than death
(If death be a deep sleep), without a groan,
Or with a cry which rather shamed my judges
Than me; but 'tis not all, for there are things
More woful—such as this small dungeon, where
I may breathe many years.

MARINA - Alas! and this
Small dungeon is all that belongs to thee

Of this wide realm, of which thy sire is Prince.

JACOPO FOSCARI - That thought would scarcely aid me to endure it.
My doom is common; many are in dungeons,
But none like mine, so near their father's palace;
But then my heart is sometimes high, and hope
Will stream along those moted rays of light
Peopled with dusty atoms, which afford
Our only day; for, save the gaoler's torch,
And a strange firefly, which was quickly caught
Last night in yon enormous spider's net,
I ne'er saw aught here like a ray. Alas!
I know if mind may bear us up, or no,
For I have such, and shown it before men;
It sinks in solitude: my soul is social.

MARINA - I will be with thee.

JACOPO FOSCARI - Ah! if it were so!
But that they never granted—nor will grant,
And I shall be alone: no men; no books—
Those lying likenesses of lying men.
I asked for even those outlines of their kind,
Which they term annals, history, what you will,
Which men bequeath as portraits, and they were
Refused me,—so these walls have been my study,
More faithful pictures of Venetian story,
With all their blank, or dismal stains, than is
The Hall not far from hence, which bears on high
Hundreds of Doges, and their deeds and dates.

MARINA - I come to tell thee the result of their
Last council on thy doom.

JACOPO FOSCARI - I know it—look!

[He points to his limbs, as referring to the Question
which he had undergone.

MARINA - No—no—no more of that: even they relent
From that atrocity.

JACOPO FOSCARI - What then?

MARINA - That you
Return to Candia.

JACOPO FOSCARI - Then my last hope's gone.
I could endure my dungeon, for 'twas Venice;
I could support the torture, there was something
In my native air that buoyed my spirits up

Like a ship on the Ocean tossed by storms,
But proudly still bestriding the high waves,
And holding on its course; but there, afar,
In that accurséd isle of slaves and captives,
And unbelievers, like a stranded wreck,
My very soul seemed mouldering in my bosom,
And piecemeal I shall perish, if remanded.

MARINA - And here?

JACOPO FOSCARI - At once—by better means, as briefer.
What! would they even deny me my Sire's sepulchre,
As well as home and heritage?

MARINA - My husband!
I have sued to accompany thee hence,
And not so hopelessly. This love of thine
For an ungrateful and tyrannic soil
Is Passion, and not Patriotism; for me,
So I could see thee with a quiet aspect,
And the sweet freedom of the earth and air,
I would not cavil about climes or regions.
This crowd of palaces and prisons is not
A Paradise; its first inhabitants
Were wretched exiles.

JACOPO FOSCARI - Well I know how wretched!

MARINA - And yet you see how, from their banishment
Before the Tartar into these salt isles,
Their antique energy of mind, all that
Remained of Rome for their inheritance,
Created by degrees an ocean Rome;
And shall an evil, which so often leads
To good, depress thee thus?

JACOPO FOSCARI - Had I gone forth
From my own land, like the old patriarchs, seeking
Another region, with their flocks and herds;
Had I been cast out like the Jews from Zion,
Or like our fathers, driven by Attila
From fertile Italy, to barren islets,
I would have given some tears to my late country
And many thoughts; but afterwards addressed
Myself, with those about me, to create
A new home and fresh state: perhaps I could
Have borne this—though I know not.

MARINA - Wherefore not?
It was the lot of millions, and must be
The fate of myriads more.

JACOPO FOSCARI - Aye—we but hear
Of the survivors' toil in their new lands,
Their numbers and success; but who can number
The hearts which broke in silence at that parting,
Or after their departure; of that malady
Which calls up green and native fields to view
From the rough deep, with such identity
To the poor exile's fevered eye, that he
Can scarcely be restrained from treading them?
That melody, which out of tones and tunes
Collects such pasture for the longing sorrow
Of the sad mountaineer, when far away
From his snow canopy of cliffs and clouds,
That he feeds on the sweet, but poisonous thought,
And dies. You call this weakness! It is strength,
I say,—the parent of all honest feeling.
He who loves not his Country, can love nothing.

MARINA - Obey her, then: 'tis she that puts thee forth.

JACOPO FOSCARI - Aye, there it is; 'tis like a mother's curse
Upon my soul—the mark is set upon me.
The exiles you speak of went forth by nations,
Their hands upheld each other by the way,
Their tents were pitched together—I'm alone.

MARINA - You shall be so no more—I will go with thee.

JACOPO FOSCARI - My best Marina!—and our children?

MARINA - They,
I fear, by the prevention of the state's
Abhorrent policy, (which holds all ties
As threads, which may be broken at her pleasure),
Will not be suffered to proceed with us.

JACOPO FOSCARI - And canst thou leave them?

MARINA - Yes—with many a pang!
But—I can leave them, children as they are,
To teach you to be less a child. From this
Learn you to sway your feelings, when exacted
By duties paramount; and 'tis our first
On earth to bear.

JACOPO FOSCARI - Have I not borne?

MARINA - Too much
From tyrannous injustice, and enough
To teach you not to shrink now from a lot,

Which, as compared with what you have undergone
Of late, is mercy.

JACOPO FOSCARI - Ah! you never yet
Were far away from Venice, never saw
Her beautiful towers in the receding distance,
While every furrow of the vessel's track
Seemed ploughing deep into your heart; you never
Saw day go down upon your native spires
So calmly with its gold and crimson glory,
And after dreaming a disturbéd vision
Of them and theirs, awoke and found them not.

MARINA - I will divide this with you. Let us think
Of our departure from this much-loved city,
(Since you must love it, as it seems,) and this
Chamber of state, her gratitude allots you.
Our children will be cared for by the Doge,
And by my uncles; we must sail ere night.

JACOPO FOSCARI - That's sudden. Shall I not behold my father?

MARINA - You will.

JACOPO FOSCARI - Where?

MARINA - Here, or in the ducal chamber—
He said not which. I would that you could bear
Your exile as he bears it.

JACOPO FOSCARI - Blame him not.
I sometimes murmur for a moment; but
He could not now act otherwise. A show
Of feeling or compassion on his part
Would have but drawn upon his agéd head
Suspicion from "the Ten," and upon mine
Accumulated ills.

MARINA - Accumulated!
What pangs are those they have spared you?

JACOPO FOSCARI - That of leaving
Venice without beholding him or you,
Which might have been forbidden now, as 'twas
Upon my former exile.

MARINA - That is true,
And thus far I am also the State's debtor,
And shall be more so when I see us both
Floating on the free waves—away—away—
Be it to the earth's end, from this abhorred,

Unjust, and—

JACOPO FOSCARI - Curse it not. If I am silent,
Who dares accuse my Country?

MARINA - Men and Angels!
The blood of myriads reeking up to Heaven,
The groans of slaves in chains, and men in dungeons,
Mothers, and wives, and sons, and sires, and subjects,
Held in the bondage of ten bald-heads; and
Though last, not least, thy silence! Couldst thou say
Aught in its favour, who would praise like thee?

JACOPO FOSCARI - Let us address us then, since so it must be,
To our departure. Who comes here?

Enter LOREDANO attended by FAMILIARS.

LOREDANO - (to the FAMILIARS) Retire,
But leave the torch.

[Exeunt the two FAMILIARS.

JACOPO FOSCARI - Most welcome, noble Signor.
I did not deem this poor place could have drawn
Such presence hither.

LOREDANO - 'Tis not the first time
I have visited these places.

MARINA - Nor would be
The last, were all men's merits well rewarded.
Came you here to insult us, or remain
As spy upon us, or as hostage for us?

LOREDANO - Neither are of my office, noble Lady!
I am sent hither to your husband, to
Announce "the Ten's" decree.

MARINA - That tenderness
Has been anticipated: it is known.

LOREDANO - As how?

MARINA - I have informed him, not so gently,
Doubtless, as your nice feelings would prescribe,
The indulgence of your colleagues; but he knew it.
If you come for our thanks, take them, and hence!
The dungeon gloom is deep enough without you,
And full of reptiles, not less loathsome, though
Their sting is honester.

JACOPO FOSCARI - I pray you, calm you:
What can avail such words?

MARINA - To let him know
That he is known.

LOREDANO - Let the fair dame preserve
Her sex's privilege.

MARINA - I have some sons, sir,
Will one day thank you better.

LOREDANO - You do well
To nurse them wisely. Foscari—you know
Your sentence, then?

JACOPO FOSCARI - Return to Candia?

LOREDANO - True—
For life.

JACOPO FOSCARI - Not long.

LOREDANO - I said—for life.

JACOPO FOSCARI - And I
Repeat—not long.

LOREDANO - A year's imprisonment
In Canea—afterwards the freedom of
The whole isle.

JACOPO FOSCARI - Both the same to me: the after
Freedom as is the first imprisonment.
Is't true my wife accompanies me?

LOREDANO - Yes,
If she so wills it.

MARINA - Who obtained that justice?

LOREDANO - One who wars not with women.

MARINA - But oppresses
Men: howsoever let him have my thanks
For the only boon I would have asked or taken
From him or such as he is.

LOREDANO - He receives them
As they are offered.

MARINA - May they thrive with him
So much!—no more.

JACOPO FOSCARI - Is this, sir, your whole mission?
Because we have brief time for preparation,
And you perceive your presence doth disquiet
This lady, of a house noble as yours.

MARINA - Nobler!

LOREDANO - How nobler?

MARINA - As more generous!
We say the "generous steed" to express the purity
Of his high blood. Thus much I've learnt, although
Venetian (who see few steeds save of bronze),
From those Venetians who have skirred the coasts
Of Egypt and her neighbour Araby:
And why not say as soon the "generous man?"
If race be aught, it is in qualities
More than in years; and mine, which is as old
As yours, is better in its product, nay—
Look not so stern—but get you back, and pore
Upon your genealogic tree's most green
Of leaves and most mature of fruits, and there
Blush to find ancestors, who would have blushed
For such a son—thou cold inveterate hater!

JACOPO FOSCARI - Again, Marina!

MARINA - Again! still, Marina.
See you not, he comes here to glut his hate
With a last look upon our misery?
Let him partake it!

JACOPO FOSCARI - That were difficult.

MARINA - Nothing more easy. He partakes it now—
Aye, he may veil beneath a marble brow
And sneering lip the pang, but he partakes it.
A few brief words of truth shame the Devil's servants
No less than Master; I have probed his soul
A moment, as the Eternal Fire, ere long,
Will reach it always. See how he shrinks from me!
With death, and chains, and exile in his hand,
To scatter o'er his kind as he thinks fit;
They are his weapons, not his armour, for
I have pierced him to the core of his cold heart.
I care not for his frowns! We can but die,
And he but live, for him the very worst

Of destinies: each day secures him more
His tempter's.

JACOPO FOSCARI - This is mere insanity.

MARINA - It may be so; and who hath made us mad?

LOREDANO - Let her go on; it irks not me.

MARINA - That's false!
You came here to enjoy a heartless triumph
Of cold looks upon manifold griefs! You came
To be sued to in vain—to mark our tears,
And hoard our groans—to gaze upon the wreck
Which you have made a Prince's son—my husband;
In short, to trample on the fallen—an office
The hangman shrinks from, as all men from him!
How have you sped? We are wretched, Signor, as
Your plots could make, and vengeance could desire us,
And how feel you?

LOREDANO - As rocks.

MARINA - By thunder blasted:
They feel not, but no less are shivered. Come,
Foscari; now let us go, and leave this felon,
The sole fit habitant of such a cell,
Which he has peopled often, but ne'er fitly
Till he himself shall brood in it alone.

Enter the DOGE.

JACOPO FOSCARI - My father!

DOGE - (embracing him). Jacopo! my son—my son!

JACOPO FOSCARI - My father still! How long it is since I
Have heard thee name my name—our name!

DOGE - My boy!
Couldst thou but know—

JACOPO FOSCARI - I rarely, sir, have murmured.

DOGE - I feel too much thou hast not.

MARINA - Doge, look there!
[She points to LOREDANO.

DOGE - I see the man—what mean'st thou?

MARINA - Caution!

LOREDANO - Being
The virtue which this noble lady most
May practise, she doth well to recommend it.

MARINA - Wretch! 'tis no virtue, but the policy
Of those who fain must deal perforce with vice:
As such I recommend it, as I would
To one whose foot was on an adder's path.

DOGE - Daughter, it is superfluous; I have long
Known Loredano.

LOREDANO - You may know him better.

MARINA - Yes; worse he could not.

JACOPO FOSCARI - Father, let not these
Our parting hours be lost in listening to
Reproaches, which boot nothing. Is it—is it,
Indeed, our last of meetings?

DOGE - You behold
These white hairs!

JACOPO FOSCARI - And I feel, besides, that mine
Will never be so white. Embrace me, father!
I loved you ever—never more than now.
Look to my children—to your last child's children:
Let them be all to you which he was once,
And never be to you what I am now.
May I not see them also?

MARINA - No—not here.

JACOPO FOSCARI - They might behold their parent any where.

MARINA - I would that they beheld their father in
A place which would not mingle fear with love,
To freeze their young blood in its natural current.
They have fed well, slept soft, and knew not that
Their sire was a mere hunted outlaw. Well,
I know his fate may one day be their heritage,
But let it only be their heritage,
And not their present fee. Their senses, though
Alive to love, are yet awake to terror;
And these vile damps, too, and yon thick green wave
Which floats above the place where we now stand—
A cell so far below the water's level,
Sending its pestilence through every crevice,

Might strike them: this is not their atmosphere,
However you—and you—and most of all,
As worthiest—you, sir, noble Loredano!
May breathe it without prejudice.

JACOPO FOSCARI - I had not
Reflected upon this, but acquiesce.
I shall depart, then, without meeting them?

DOGE - Not so: they shall await you in my chamber.

JACOPO FOSCARI - And must I leave them—all?

LOREDANO - You must.

JACOPO FOSCARI - Not one?

LOREDANO - They are the State's.

MARINA - I thought they had been mine.

LOREDANO - They are, in all maternal things.

MARINA - That is,
In all things painful. If they're sick, they will
Be left to me to tend them; should they die,
To me to bury and to mourn; but if
They live, they'll make you soldiers, senators,
Slaves, exiles—what you will; or if they are
Females with portions, brides and bribes for nobles!
Behold the State's care for its sons and mothers!

LOREDANO - The hour approaches, and the wind is fair.

JACOPO FOSCARI - How know you that here, where the genial wind
Ne'er blows in all its blustering freedom?

LOREDANO - 'Twas so
When I came here. The galley floats within
A bow-shot of the "Riva di Schiavoni."

JACOPO FOSCARI - Father! I pray you to precede me, and
Prepare my children to behold their father.

DOGE - Be firm, my son!

JACOPO FOSCARI - I will do my endeavour.

MARINA - Farewell! at least to this detested dungeon,
And him to whose good offices you owe
In part your past imprisonment.

LOREDANO - And present
Liberation.

DOGE - He speaks truth.

JACOPO FOSCARI - No doubt! but 'tis
Exchange of chains for heavier chains I owe him.
He knows this, or he had not sought to change them,
But I reproach not.

LOREDANO - The time narrows, Signor.

JACOPO FOSCARI - Alas! I little thought so lingeringly
To leave abodes like this: but when I feel
That every step I take, even from this cell,
Is one away from Venice, I look back
Even on these dull damp walls, and—

DOGE - Boy! no tears.

MARINA - Let them flow on: he wept not on the rack
To shame him, and they cannot shame him now.
They will relieve his heart—that too kind heart—
And I will find an hour to wipe away
Those tears, or add my own. I could weep now,
But would not gratify yon wretch so far.
Let us proceed. Doge, lead the way.

LOREDANO - (to the FAMILIAR) The torch, there!

MARINA - Yes, light us on, as to a funeral pyre,
With Loredano mourning like an heir.

DOGE - My son, you are feeble; take this hand.

JACOPO FOSCARI - Alas!
Must youth support itself on age, and I
Who ought to be the prop of yours?

LOREDANO - Take mine.

MARINA - Touch it not, Foscari; 'twill sting you. Signor,
Stand off! be sure, that if a grasp of yours
Would raise us from the gulf wherein we are plunged,
No hand of ours would stretch itself to meet it.
Come, Foscari, take the hand the altar gave you;
It could not save, but will support you ever.

[Exeunt.

ACT IV

SCENE I. A Hall in the Ducal Palace.

Enter LOREDANO and BARBARIGO.

BARBARIGO - And have you confidence in such a project?

LOREDANO - I have.

BARBARIGO - 'Tis hard upon his years.

LOREDANO - Say rather
Kind to relieve him from the cares of State.

BARBARIGO - 'Twill break his heart.

LOREDANO - Age has no heart to break.
He has seen his son's half broken, and, except
A start of feeling in his dungeon, never
Swerved.

BARBARIGO - In his countenance, I grant you, never;
But I have seen him sometimes in a calm
So desolate, that the most clamorous grief
Had nought to envy him within. Where is he?

LOREDANO - In his own portion of the palace, with
His son, and the whole race of Foscaris.

BARBARIGO - Bidding farewell.

LOREDANO - A last! as, soon, he shall
Bid to his Dukedom.

BARBARIGO - When embarks the son?

LOREDANO - Forthwith—when this long leave is taken. 'Tis
Time to admonish them again.

BARBARIGO - Forbear;
Retrench not from their moments.

LOREDANO - Not I, now
We have higher business for our own. This day
Shall be the last of the old Doge's reign,
As the first of his son's last banishment,
And that is vengeance.

BARBARIGO - In my mind, too deep.

LOREDANO - 'Tis moderate—not even life for life, the rule
Denounced of retribution from all time;
They owe me still my father's and my uncle's.

BARBARIGO - Did not the Doge deny this strongly?

LOREDANO - Doubtless.

BARBARIGO - And did not this shake your suspicion?

LOREDANO - No.

BARBARIGO - But if this deposition should take place
By our united influence in the Council,
It must be done with all the deference
Due to his years, his station, and his deeds.

LOREDANO - As much of ceremony as you will,
So that the thing be done. You may, for aught
I care, depute the Council on their knees,
(Like Barbarossa to the Pope,) to beg him
To have the courtesy to abdicate.

BARBARIGO - What if he will not?

LOREDANO - We'll elect another,
And make him null.

BARBARIGO - But will the laws uphold us?

LOREDANO - What laws?—"The Ten" are laws; and if they were not,
I will be legislator in this business.

BARBARIGO - At your own peril?

LOREDANO - There is none, I tell you,
Our powers are such.

BARBARIGO - But he has twice already
Solicited permission to retire,
And twice it was refused.

LOREDANO - The better reason
To grant it the third time.

BARBARIGO - Unasked?

LOREDANO - It shows

The impression of his former instances:
If they were from his heart, he may be thankful:
If not, 'twill punish his hypocrisy.
Come, they are met by this time; let us join them,
And be thou fixed in purpose for this once.
I have prepared such arguments as will not
Fail to move them, and to remove him: since
Their thoughts, their objects, have been sounded, do not
You, with your wonted scruples, teach us pause,
And all will prosper.

BARBARIGO - Could I but be certain
This is no prelude to such persecution
Of the sire as has fallen upon the son,
I would support you.

LOREDANO - He is safe, I tell you;
His fourscore years and five may linger on
As long as he can drag them: 'tis his throne
Alone is aimed at.

BARBARIGO - But discarded Princes
Are seldom long of life.

LOREDANO - And men of eighty
More seldom still.

BARBARIGO - And why not wait these few years?

LOREDANO - Because we have waited long enough, and he
Lived longer than enough. Hence! in to council!
[Exeunt LOREDANO and BARBARIGO.

Enter MEMMO and a Senator.

SENATOR - A summons to "the Ten!" why so?

MEMMO - "The Ten"
Alone can answer; they are rarely wont
To let their thoughts anticipate their purpose
By previous proclamation. We are summoned—
That is enough.

SENATOR - For them, but not for us;
I would know why.

MEMMO - You will know why anon,
If you obey: and, if not, you no less
Will know why you should have obeyed.

SENATOR - I mean not

To oppose them, but—

MEMMO - In Venice "but"'s a traitor.
But me no "buts" unless you would pass o'er
The Bridge which few repass.

SENATOR - I am silent.

MEMMO - Why
Thus hesitate? "The Ten" have called in aid
Of their deliberation five and twenty
Patricians of the Senate—you are one,
And I another; and it seems to me
Both honoured by the choice or chance which leads us
To mingle with a body so august.

SENATOR - Most true. I say no more.

MEMMO - As we hope, Signor,
And all may honestly, (that is, all those
Of noble blood may,) one day hope to be
Decemvir, it is surely for the Senate's
Chosen delegates, a school of wisdom, to
Be thus admitted, though as novices,
To view the mysteries.

SENATOR - Let us view them: they,
No doubt, are worth it.

MEMMO - Being worth our lives
If we divulge them, doubtless they are worth
Something, at least to you or me.

SENATOR - I sought not
A place within the sanctuary; but being
Chosen, however reluctantly so chosen,
I shall fulfil my office.

MEMMO - Let us not
Be latest in obeying "the Ten's" summons.

SENATOR - All are not met, but I am of your thought
So far—let's in.

MEMMO - The earliest are most welcome
In earnest councils—we will not be least so.

[Exeunt.

Enter the DOGE, JACOPO FOSCARI, and MARINA.

JACOPO FOSCARI - Ah, father! though I must and will depart,
Yet—yet—I pray you to obtain for me
That I once more return unto my home,
Howe'er remote the period. Let there be
A point of time, as beacon to my heart,
With any penalty annexed they please,
But let me still return.

DOGE - Son Jacopo,
Go and obey our Country's will: 'tis not
For us to look beyond.

JACOPO FOSCARI - But still I must
Look back. I pray you think of me.

DOGE - Alas!
You ever were my dearest offspring, when
They were more numerous, nor can be less so
Now you are last; but did the State demand
The exile of the disinterréd ashes
Of your three goodly brothers, now in earth,
And their desponding shades came flitting round
To impede the act, I must no less obey
A duty, paramount to every duty.

MARINA - My husband! let us on: this but prolongs
Our sorrow.

JACOPO FOSCARI - But we are not summoned yet;
The galley's sails are not unfurled:—who knows?
The wind may change.

MARINA - And if it do, it will not
Change their hearts, or your lot: the galley's oars
Will quickly clear the harbour.

JACOPO FOSCARI - O, ye Elements!
Where are your storms?

MARINA - In human breasts. Alas!
Will nothing calm you?

JACOPO FOSCARI - Never yet did mariner
Put up to patron saint such prayers for prosperous
And pleasant breezes, as I call upon you,
Ye tutelar saints of my own city! which
Ye love not with more holy love than I,
To lash up from the deep the Adrian waves,
And waken Auster, sovereign of the Tempest!
Till the sea dash me back on my own shore
A broken corse upon the barren Lido,

Where I may mingle with the sands which skirt
The land I love, and never shall see more!

MARINA - And wish you this with me beside you?

JACOPO FOSCARI - No—
No—not for thee, too good, too kind! May'st thou
Live long to be a mother to those children
Thy fond fidelity for a time deprives
Of such support! But for myself alone,
May all the winds of Heaven howl down the Gulf,
And tear the vessel, till the mariners,
Appalled, turn their despairing eyes on me,
As the Phenicians did on Jonah, then
Cast me out from amongst them, as an offering
To appease the waves. The billow which destroys me
Will be more merciful than man, and bear me
Dead, but still bear me to a native grave,
From fishers' hands, upon the desolate strand,
Which, of its thousand wrecks, hath ne'er received
One lacerated like the heart which then
Will be.—But wherefore breaks it not? why live I?

MARINA - To man thyself, I trust, with time, to master
Such useless passion. Until now thou wert
A sufferer, but not a loud one: why
What is this to the things thou hast borne in silence—
Imprisonment and actual torture?

JACOPO FOSCARI - Double,
Triple, and tenfold torture! But you are right,
It must be borne. Father, your blessing.

DOGE - Would
It could avail thee! but no less thou hast it.

JACOPO FOSCARI - Forgive—

DOGE - What?

JACOPO FOSCARI - My poor mother, for my birth,
And me for having lived, and you yourself
(As I forgive you), for the gift of life,
Which you bestowed upon me as my sire.

MARINA - What hast thou done?

JACOPO FOSCARI - Nothing. I cannot charge
My memory with much save sorrow: but
I have been so beyond the common lot
Chastened and visited, I needs must think

That I was wicked. If it be so, may
What I have undergone here keep me from
A like hereafter!

MARINA - Fear not: that's reserved
For your oppressors.

JACOPO FOSCARI - Let me hope not.

MARINA - Hope not?

JACOPO FOSCARI - I cannot wish them all they have inflicted.

MARINA - All! the consummate fiends! A thousandfold
May the worm which never dieth feed upon them!

JACOPO FOSCARI - They may repent.

MARINA - And if they do, Heaven will not
Accept the tardy penitence of demons.

Enter an OFFICER and Guards.

OFFICER - Signor! the boat is at the shore—the wind
Is rising—we are ready to attend you.

JACOPO FOSCARI - And I to be attended. Once more, father,
Your hand!

DOGE - Take it. Alas! how thine own trembles!

JACOPO FOSCARI - No—you mistake; 'tis yours that shakes, my father.
Farewell!

DOGE - Farewell! Is there aught else?

JACOPO FOSCARI - No—nothing.
[To the OFFICER.
Lend me your arm, good Signor.

OFFICER - You turn pale—
Let me support you—paler—ho! some aid there!
Some water!

MARINA - Ah, he is dying!

JACOPO FOSCARI - Now, I'm ready—
My eyes swim strangely—where's the door?

MARINA - Away!
Let me support him—my best love! Oh, God!

How faintly beats this heart—this pulse!

JACOPO FOSCARI - The light!
Is it the light?—I am faint.

[OFFICER presents him with water.

OFFICER - He will be better,
Perhaps, in the air.

JACOPO FOSCARI - I doubt not. Father—wife—
Your hands!

MARINA - There's death in that damp, clammy grasp.
Oh, God!—My Foscari, how fare you?

JACOPO FOSCARI - Well!

[He dies.

OFFICER - He's gone!

DOGE - He's free.

MARINA - No—no, he is not dead;
There must be life yet in that heart—he could not
Thus leave me.

DOGE - Daughter!

MARINA - Hold thy peace, old man!
I am no daughter now—thou hast no son.
Oh, Foscari!

OFFICER - We must remove the body.

MARINA - Touch it not, dungeon miscreants! your base office
Ends with his life, and goes not beyond murder,
Even by your murderous laws. Leave his remains
To those who know to honour them.

OFFICER - I must
Inform the Signory, and learn their pleasure.

DOGE - Inform the Signory from me, the Doge,
They have no further power upon those ashes:
While he lived, he was theirs, as fits a subject—
Now he is mine—my broken-hearted boy!

[Exit OFFICER.

MARINA - And I must live!

DOGE - Your children live, Marina.

MARINA - My children! true—they live, and I must live
To bring them up to serve the State, and die
As died their father. Oh! what best of blessings
Were barrenness in Venice! Would my mother
Had been so!

DOGE - My unhappy children!

MARINA - What!
You feel it then at last—you!—Where is now
The Stoic of the State?

DOGE - (throwing himself down by the body). Here!

MARINA - Aye, weep on!
I thought you had no tears—you hoarded them
Until they are useless; but weep on! he never
Shall weep more—never, never more.

Enter LOREDANO and BARBARIGO.

LOREDANO - What's here?

MARINA - Ah! the Devil come to insult the dead! Avaunt!
Incarnate Lucifer! 'tis holy ground.
A martyr's ashes now lie there, which make it
A shrine. Get thee back to thy place of torment!

BARBARIGO - Lady, we knew not of this sad event,
But passed here merely on our path from council.

MARINA - Pass on.

LOREDANO - We sought the Doge.

MARINA - (pointing to the Doge, who is still on the ground
by his son's body) He's busy, look,
About the business you provided for him.
Are ye content?

BARBARIGO - We will not interrupt
A parent's sorrows.

MARINA - No, ye only make them,
Then leave them.

DOGE - (rising). Sirs, I am ready.

BARBARIGO - No—not now.

LOREDANO - Yet 'twas important.

DOGE - If 'twas so, I can
Only repeat—I am ready.

BARBARIGO - It shall not be
Just now, though Venice tottered o'er the deep
Like a frail vessel. I respect your griefs.

DOGE - I thank you. If the tidings which you bring
Are evil, you may say them; nothing further
Can touch me more than him thou look'st on there;
If they be good, say on; you need not fear
That they can comfort me.

BARBARIGO - I would they could!

DOGE - I spoke not to you, but to Loredano.
He understands me.

MARINA - Ah! I thought it would be so.

DOGE - What mean you?

MARINA - Lo! there is the blood beginning
To flow through the dead lips of Foscari—
The body bleeds in presence of the assassin.
[To LOREDANO.
Thou cowardly murderer by law, behold
How Death itself bears witness to thy deeds!

DOGE - My child! this is a phantasy of grief.
Bear hence the body. [To his ATTENDANTS] Signors, if it please you,
Within an hour I'll hear you.

[Exeunt DOGE, MARINA, and attendants with the body.

[Enter LOREDANO and BARBARIGO.

BARBARIGO - He must not
Be troubled now.

LOREDANO - He said himself that nought
Could give him trouble farther.

BARBARIGO - These are words;
But Grief is lonely, and the breaking in
Upon it barbarous.

LOREDANO - Sorrow preys upon
Its solitude, and nothing more diverts it
From its sad visions of the other world,
Than calling it at moments back to this.
The busy have no time for tears.

BARBARIGO - And therefore
You would deprive this old man of all business?

LOREDANO - The thing's decreed. The Giunta and "the Ten"
Have made it law—who shall oppose that law?

BARBARIGO - Humanity!

LOREDANO - Because his son is dead?

BARBARIGO - And yet unburied.

LOREDANO - Had we known this when
The act was passing, it might have suspended
Its passage, but impedes it not—once passed.

BARBARIGO - I'll not consent.

LOREDANO - You have consented to
All that's essential—leave the rest to me.

BARBARIGO - Why press his abdication now?

LOREDANO - The feelings
Of private passion may not interrupt
The public benefit; and what the State
Decides to-day must not give way before
To-morrow for a natural accident.

BARBARIGO - You have a son.

LOREDANO - I have—and had a father.

BARBARIGO - Still so inexorable?

LOREDANO - Still.

BARBARIGO - But let him
Inter his son before we press upon him
This edict.

LOREDANO - Let him call up into life
My sire and uncle—I consent. Men may,
Even agéd men, be, or appear to be,

Sires of a hundred sons, but cannot kindle
An atom of their ancestors from earth.
The victims are not equal; he has seen
His sons expire by natural deaths, and I
My sires by violent and mysterious maladies.
I used no poison, bribed no subtle master
Of the destructive art of healing, to
Shorten the path to the eternal cure.
His sons—and he had four—are dead, without
My dabbling in vile drugs.

BARBARIGO - And art thou sure
He dealt in such?

LOREDANO - Most sure.

BARBARIGO - And yet he seems
All openness.

LOREDANO - And so he seemed not long
Ago to Carmagnuola.

BARBARIGO - The attainted
And foreign traitor?

LOREDANO - Even so: when he,
After the very night in which "the Ten"
(Joined with the Doge) decided his destruction,
Met the great Duke at daybreak with a jest,
Demanding whether he should augur him
"The good day or good night?" his Doge-ship answered,
"That he in truth had passed a night of vigil,
In which" (he added with a gracious smile)
"There often has been question about you."
'Twas true; the question was the death resolved
Of Carmagnuola, eight months ere he died;
And the old Doge, who knew him doomed, smiled on him
With deadly cozenage, eight long months beforehand—
Eight months of such hypocrisy as is
Learnt but in eighty years. Brave Carmagnuola
Is dead; so is young Foscari and his brethren—
I never smiled on them.

BARBARIGO - Was Carmagnuola
Your friend?

LOREDANO - He was the safeguard of the city.
In early life its foe, but in his manhood,
Its saviour first, then victim.

BARBARIGO - Ah! that seems

The penalty of saving cities. He
Whom we now act against not only saved
Our own, but added others to her sway.

LOREDANO - The Romans (and we ape them) gave a crown
To him who took a city: and they gave
A crown to him who saved a citizen
In battle: the rewards are equal. Now,
If we should measure forth the cities taken
By the Doge Foscari, with citizens
Destroyed by him, or through him, the account
Were fearfully against him, although narrowed
To private havoc, such as between him
And my dead father.

BARBARIGO - Are you then thus fixed?

LOREDANO - Why, what should change me?

BARBARIGO - That which changes me.
But you, I know, are marble to retain
A feud. But when all is accomplished, when
The old man is deposed, his name degraded,
His sons all dead, his family depressed,
And you and yours triumphant, shall you sleep?

LOREDANO - More soundly.

BARBARIGO - That's an error, and you'll find it
Ere you sleep with your fathers.

LOREDANO - They sleep not
In their accelerated graves, nor will
Till Foscari fills his. Each night I see them
Stalk frowning round my couch, and, pointing towards
The ducal palace, marshal me to vengeance.

BARBARIGO - Fancy's distemperature! There is no passion
More spectral or fantastical than Hate;
Not even its opposite, Love, so peoples air
With phantoms, as this madness of the heart.

Enter an OFFICER.

LOREDANO - Where go you, sirrah?

OFFICER - By the ducal order
To forward the preparatory rites
For the late Foscari's interment.

BARBARIGO - Their

Vault has been often opened of late years.

LOREDANO - 'Twill be full soon, and may be closed for ever!

OFFICER - May I pass on?

LOREDANO - You may.

BARBARIGO - How bears the Doge
This last calamity?

OFFICER - With desperate firmness.
In presence of another he says little,
But I perceive his lips move now and then;
And once or twice I heard him, from the adjoining
Apartment, mutter forth the words—"My son!"
Scarce audibly. I must proceed.

[Exit OFFICER.

BARBARIGO - This stroke
Will move all Venice in his favour.

LOREDANO - Right!
We must be speedy: let us call together
The delegates appointed to convey
The Council's resolution.

BARBARIGO - I protest
Against it at this moment.

LOREDANO - As you please—
I'll take their voices on it ne'ertheless,
And see whose most may sway them, yours or mine.

[Exeunt BARBARIGO and LOREDANO.

ACT V

SCENE I. The Doge's Apartment.

The DOGE and Attendants.

ATTENDANT - My Lord, the deputation is in waiting;
But add, that if another hour would better
Accord with your will, they will make it theirs.

DOGE - To me all hours are like. Let them approach.

[Exit ATTENDANT.

An OFFICER - Prince! I have done your bidding.

DOGE - What command?

OFFICER - A melancholy one—to call the attendance
Of—

DOGE - True—true—true: I crave your pardon. I
Begin to fail in apprehension, and
Wax very old—old almost as my years.
Till now I fought them off, but they begin
To overtake me.

Enter the Deputation, consisting of six of the Signory and the CHIEF OF THE TEN.

Noble men, your pleasure!

CHIEF OF THE TEN - In the first place, the Council doth condole
With the Doge on his late and private grief.

DOGE - No more—no more of that.

CHIEF OF THE TEN - Will not the Duke
Accept the homage of respect?

DOGE - I do
Accept it as 'tis given—proceed.

CHIEF OF THE TEN - "The Ten,"
With a selected giunta from the Senate
Of twenty-five of the best born patricians,
Having deliberated on the state
Of the Republic, and the o'erwhelming cares
Which, at this moment, doubly must oppress
Your years, so long devoted to your Country,
Have judged it fitting, with all reverence,
Now to solicit from your wisdom (which
Upon reflection must accord in this),
The resignation of the ducal ring,
Which you have worn so long and venerably:
And to prove that they are not ungrateful, nor
Cold to your years and services, they add
An appanage of twenty hundred golden
Ducats, to make retirement not less splendid
Than should become a Sovereign's retreat.

DOGE - Did I hear rightly?

CHIEF OF THE TEN - Need I say again?

DOGE - No.—Have you done?

CHIEF OF THE TEN - I have spoken. Twenty four
Hours are accorded you to give an answer.

DOGE - I shall not need so many seconds.

CHIEF OF THE TEN - Will now retire.

DOGE - Stay! four and twenty hours
Will alter nothing which I have to say.

CHIEF OF THE TEN - Speak!

DOGE - When I twice before reiterated
My wish to abdicate, it was refused me:
And not alone refused, but ye exacted
An oath from me that I would never more
Renew this instance. I have sworn to die
In full exertion of the functions, which
My Country called me here to exercise,
According to my honour and my conscience—
I cannot break my oath.

CHIEF OF THE TEN - Reduce us not
To the alternative of a decree,
Instead of your compliance.

DOGE - Providence
Prolongs my days to prove and chasten me;
But ye have no right to reproach my length
Of days, since every hour has been the Country's.
I am ready to lay down my life for her,
As I have laid down dearer things than life:
But for my dignity—I hold it of
The whole Republic: when the general will
Is manifest, then you shall all be answered.

CHIEF OF THE TEN - We grieve for such an answer; but it cannot
Avail you aught.

DOGE - I can submit to all things,
But nothing will advance; no, not a moment.
What you decree—decree.

CHIEF OF THE TEN - With this, then, must we
Return to those who sent us?

DOGE - You have heard me.

CHIEF OF THE TEN - With all due reverence we retire.
[Exeunt the Deputation, etc.

Enter an ATTENDANT.

ATTENDANT - My Lord,
The noble dame Marina craves an audience.

DOGE - My time is hers.

Enter MARINA.

MARINA - My Lord, if I intrude—
Perhaps you fain would be alone?

DOGE - Alone!
Alone, come all the world around me, I
Am now and evermore. But we will bear it.

MARINA - We will, and for the sake of those who are,
Endeavour—Oh, my husband!

DOGE - Give it way:
I cannot comfort thee.

MARINA - He might have lived,
So formed for gentle privacy of life,
So loving, so beloved; the native of
Another land, and who so blest and blessing
As my poor Foscari? Nothing was wanting
Unto his happiness and mine save not
To be Venetian.

DOGE - Or a Prince's son.

MARINA - Yes; all things which conduce to other men's
Imperfect happiness or high ambition,
By some strange destiny, to him proved deadly.
The Country and the People whom he loved,
The Prince of whom he was the elder born,
And—

DOGE - Soon may be a Prince no longer.

MARINA - How?

DOGE - They have taken my son from me, and now aim
At my too long worn diadem and ring.
Let them resume the gewgaws!

MARINA - Oh, the tyrants!
In such an hour too!

DOGE - 'Tis the fittest time;
An hour ago I should have felt it.

MARINA - And
Will you not now resent it?—Oh, for vengeance!
But he, who, had he been enough protected,
Might have repaid protection in this moment,
Cannot assist his father.

DOGE - Nor should do so
Against his Country, had he a thousand lives
Instead of that—

MARINA - They tortured from him. This
May be pure patriotism. I am a woman:
To me my husband and my children were
Country and home. I loved him—how I loved him!
I have seen him pass through such an ordeal as
The old martyrs would have shrunk from: he is gone,
And I, who would have given my blood for him,
Have nought to give but tears! But could I compass
The retribution of his wrongs!—Well, well!
I have sons, who shall be men.

DOGE - Your grief distracts you.

MARINA - I thought I could have borne it, when I saw him
Bowed down by such oppression; yes, I thought
That I would rather look upon his corpse
Than his prolonged captivity:—I am punished
For that thought now. Would I were in his grave!

DOGE - I must look on him once more.

MARINA - Come with me!

DOGE - Is he—

MARINA - Our bridal bed is now his bier,

DOGE - And he is in his shroud!

MARINA - Come, come, old man!

[Exeunt the DOGE and MARINA.

Enter BARBARIGO and LOREDANO.

BARBARIGO - (to an Attendant). Where is the Doge?

ATTENDANT - This instant retired hence,
With the illustrious lady his son's widow.

LOREDANO - Where?

ATTENDANT - To the chamber where the body lies.

BARBARIGO - Let us return, then.

LOREDANO - You forget, you cannot.
We have the implicit order of the Giunta
To await their coming here, and join them in
Their office: they'll be here soon after us.

BARBARIGO - And will they press their answer on the Doge?

LOREDANO - 'Twas his own wish that all should be done promptly.
He answered quickly, and must so be answered;
His dignity is looked to, his estate
Cared for—what would he more?

BARBARIGO - Die in his robes:
He could not have lived long; but I have done
My best to save his honours, and opposed
This proposition to the last, though vainly.
Why would the general vote compel me hither?

LOREDANO - 'Twas fit that some one of such different thoughts
From ours should be a witness, lest false tongues
Should whisper that a harsh majority
Dreaded to have its acts beheld by others.

BARBARIGO - And not less, I must needs think, for the sake
Of humbling me for my vain opposition.
You are ingenious, Loredano, in
Your modes of vengeance, nay, poetical,
A very Ovid in the art of hating;
'Tis thus (although a secondary object,
Yet hate has microscopic eyes), to you
I owe, by way of foil to the more zealous,
This undesired association in
Your Giunta's duties.

LOREDANO - How!—my Giunta!

BARBARIGO - Yours!
They speak your language, watch your nod, approve
Your plans, and do your work. Are they not yours?

LOREDANO - You talk unwarily. 'Twere best they hear not
This from you.

BARBARIGO - Oh! they'll hear as much one day
From louder tongues than mine; they have gone beyond
Even their exorbitance of power: and when
This happens in the most contemned and abject
States, stung humanity will rise to check it.

LOREDANO - You talk but idly.

BARBARIGO - That remains for proof.
Here come our colleagues.

Enter the Deputation as before.

CHIEF OF THE TEN - Is the Duke aware
We seek his presence?

ATTENDANT - He shall be informed.

[Exit ATTENDANT.

BARBARIGO - The Duke is with his son.

CHIEF OF THE TEN - If it be so,
We will remit him till the rites are over.
Let us return. 'Tis time enough to-morrow.

LOREDANO - (aside to BARBARGIO)
Now the rich man's hell-fire upon your tongue,
Unquenched, unquenchable! I'll have it torn
From its vile babbling roots, till you shall utter
Nothing but sobs through blood, for this! Sage Signors,
I pray ye be not hasty.   [Aloud to the others.

BARBARIGO - But be human!

LOREDANO - See, the Duke comes!

Enter the DOGE.

DOGE - I have obeyed your summons.

CHIEF OF THE TEN - We come once more to urge our past request.

DOGE - And I to answer.

CHIEF OF THE TEN - What?

DOGE - My only answer.

You have heard it.

CHIEF OF THE TEN - Hear you then the last decree,
Definitive and absolute!

DOGE - To the point—
To the point! I know of old the forms of office,
And gentle preludes to strong acts.—Go on!

CHIEF OF THE TEN - You are no longer Doge; you are released
From your imperial oath as Sovereign;
Your ducal robes must be put off; but for
Your services, the State allots the appanage
Already mentioned in our former congress.
Three days are left you to remove from hence,
Under the penalty to see confiscated
All your own private fortune.

DOGE - That last clause,
I am proud to say, would not enrich the treasury.

CHIEF OF THE TEN - Your answer, Duke!

LOREDANO - Your answer, Francis Foscari!

DOGE - If I could have foreseen that my old age
Was prejudicial to the State, the Chief
Of the Republic never would have shown
Himself so far ungrateful, as to place
His own high dignity before his Country;
But this life having been so many years
Not useless to that Country, I would fain
Have consecrated my last moments to her.
But the decree being rendered, I obey.

CHIEF OF THE TEN - If you would have the three days named extended,
We willingly will lengthen them to eight,
As sign of our esteem.

DOGE - Not eight hours, Signor,
Not even eight minutes—there's the ducal ring,

[Taking off his ring and cap.

And there the ducal diadem! And so
The Adriatic's free to wed another.

CHIEF OF THE TEN - Yet go not forth so quickly.

DOGE - I am old, sir,
And even to move but slowly must begin

To move betimes. Methinks I see amongst you
A face I know not.—Senator! your name,
You, by your garb, Chief of the Forty!

MEMMO - Signor,
I am the son of Marco Memmo.

DOGE - Ah!
Your father was my friend.—But sons and fathers!—
What, ho! my servants there!

ATTENDANT - My Prince!

DOGE - No Prince—
There are the princes of the Prince!
[Pointing to the Ten's Deputation
—Prepare
To part from hence upon the instant.

CHIEF OF THE TEN - Why
So rashly? 'twill give scandal.

DOGE - (to the TEN) - Answer that;
It is your province.
[To the SERVANTE.
—Sirs, bestir yourselves:
There is one burthen which I beg you bear
With care, although 'tis past all farther harm—
But I will look to that myself.

BARBARIGO - He means
The body of his son.

DOGE - And call Marina,
My daughter!

Enter MARINA.

DOGE - Get thee ready, we must mourn
Elsewhere.

MARINA - And everywhere.

DOGE - True; but in freedom,
Without these jealous spies upon the great.
Signers, you may depart: what would you more?
We are going; do you fear that we shall bear
The palace with us? Its old walls, ten times
As old as I am, and I'm very old,
Have served you, so have I, and I and they
Could tell a tale; but I invoke them not

To fall upon you! else they would, as erst
The pillars of stone Dagon's temple on
The Israelite and his Philistine foes.
Such power I do believe there might exist
In such a curse as mine, provoked by such
As you; but I curse not. Adieu, good Signers!
May the next Duke be better than the present!

LOREDANO - The present Duke is Paschal Malipiero.

DOGE - Not till I pass the threshold of these doors.

LOREDANO - Saint Mark's great bell is soon about to toll
For his inauguration.

DOGE - Earth and Heaven!
Ye will reverberate this peal; and I
Live to hear this!—the first Doge who e'er heard
Such sound for his successor: happier he,
My attainted predecessor, stern Faliero—
This insult at the least was spared him.

LOREDANO - What!
Do you regret a traitor?

DOGE - No—I merely
Envy the dead.

CHIEF OF THE TEN - My Lord, if you indeed
Are bent upon this rash abandonment
Of the State's palace, at the least retire
By the private staircase, which conducts you towards
The landing-place of the canal.

DOGE - No. I
Will now descend the stairs by which I mounted
To sovereignty—the Giants' Stairs, on whose
Broad eminence I was invested Duke.
My services have called me up those steps,
The malice of my foes will drive me down them.
There five and thirty years ago was I
Installed, and traversed these same halls, from which
I never thought to be divorced except
A corse—a corse, it might be, fighting for them—
But not pushed hence by fellow-citizens.
But come; my son and I will go together—
He to his grave, and I to pray for mine.

CHIEF OF THE TEN - What! thus in public?

DOGE - I was publicly

Elected, and so will I be deposed.
Marina! art thou willing?

MARINA - Here's my arm!

DOGE - And here my staff: thus propped will I go forth.

CHIEF OF THE TEN - It must not be—the people will perceive it.

DOGE - The people,—There's no people, you well know it,
Else you dare not deal thus by them or me.
There is a populace, perhaps, whose looks
May shame you; but they dare not groan nor curse you,
Save with their hearts and eyes.

CHIEF OF THE TEN - you speak in passion,
Else—

DOGE - You have reason. I have spoken much
More than my wont: it is a foible which
Was not of mine, but more excuses you,
Inasmuch as it shows, that I approach
A dotage which may justify this deed
Of yours, although the law does not, nor will.
Farewell, sirs!

BARBARIGO - You shall not depart without
An escort fitting past and present rank.
We will accompany, with due respect,
The Doge unto his private palace. Say!
My brethren, will we not?

DIFFERENT VOICES - Aye!—Aye!

DOGE - You shall not
Stir—in my train, at least. I entered here
As Sovereign—I go out as citizen
By the same portals, but as citizen.
All these vain ceremonies are base insults,
Which only ulcerate the heart the more,
Applying poisons there as antidotes.
Pomp is for Princes—I am none!—That's false,
I am, but only to these gates.—Ah!

LOREDANO - Hark!

[The great bell of St. Mark's tolls.

BARBARIGO - The bell!

CHIEF OF THE TEN - St. Mark's, which tolls for the election

Of Malipiero.

DOGE - Well I recognise
The sound! I heard it once, but once before,
And that is five and thirty years ago;
Even then I was not young.

BARBARIGO - Sit down, my Lord!
You tremble.

DOGE - 'Tis the knell of my poor boy!
My heart aches bitterly.

BARBARIGO - I pray you sit.

DOGE - No; my seat here has been a throne till now.
Marina! let us go.

MARINA - Most readily.

DOGE - (walks a few steps, then stops).
I feel athirst—will no one bring me here
A cup of water?

BARBARIGO - I—

MARINA - And I—

LOREDANO - And I—
[The DOGE takes a goblet from the hand of LOREDANO.

DOGE - I take yours, Loredano, from the hand
Most fit for such an hour as this.

LOREDANO - Why so?

DOGE - 'Tis said that our Venetian crystal has
Such pure antipathy to poisons as
To burst, if aught of venom touches it.
You bore this goblet, and it is not broken.

LOREDANO - Well, sir!

DOGE - Then it is false, or you are true.
For my own part, I credit neither; 'tis
An idle legend.

MARINA - You talk wildly, and
Had better now be seated, nor as yet
Depart. Ah! now you look as looked my husband!

BARBARIGO - He sinks!—support him!—quick—a chair—support him!

DOGE - The bell tolls on!—let's hence—my brain's on fire!

BARBARIGO - I do beseech you, lean upon us!

DOGE - No!
A Sovereign should die standing. My poor boy!
Off with your arms!—That bell!

[The DOGE drops down and dies.

MARINA - My God! My God!

BARBARIGO - (to LOREDANO). Behold! your work's completed!

CHIEF OF THE TEN - Is there then
No aid? Call in assistance!

ATTENDANT - 'Tis all over.

CHIEF OF THE TEN - If it be so, at least his obsequies
Shall be such as befits his name and nation,
His rank and his devotion to the duties
Of the realm, while his age permitted him
To do himself and them full justice. Brethren,
Say, shall it not be so?

BARBARIGO - He has not had
The misery to die a subject where
He reigned: then let his funeral rites be princely.

CHIEF OF THE TEN - We are agreed, then?

ALL except LOREDANO, answer - Yes.

CHIEF OF THE TEN - Heaven's peace be with him!

MARINA - Signers, your pardon: this is mockery.
Juggle no more with that poor remnant, which,
A moment since, while yet it had a soul,
(A soul by whom you have increased your Empire,
And made your power as proud as was his glory),
You banished from his palace and tore down
From his high place, with such relentless coldness;
And now, when he can neither know these honours,
Nor would accept them if he could, you, Signors,
Purpose, with idle and superfluous pomp,
To make a pageant over what you trampled.
A princely funeral will be your reproach,
And not his honour.

CHIEF OF THE TEN - Lady, we revoke not
Our purposes so readily.

MARINA - I know it,
As far as touches torturing the living.
I thought the dead had been beyond even you,
Though (some, no doubt) consigned to powers which may
Resemble that you exercise on earth.
Leave him to me; you would have done so for
His dregs of life, which you have kindly shortened:
It is my last of duties, and may prove
A dreary comfort in my desolation.
Grief is fantastical, and loves the dead,
And the apparel of the grave.

CHIEF OF THE TEN - Do you
Pretend still to this office?

MARINA - I do, Signor.
Though his possessions have been all consumed
In the State's service, I have still my dowry,
Which shall be consecrated to his rites,
And those of—

[She stops with agitation.

CHIEF OF THE TEN - Best retain it for your children.

MARINA - Aye, they are fatherless, I thank you.

CHIEF OF THE TEN - We
Cannot comply with your request. His relics
Shall be exposed with wonted pomp, and followed
Unto their home by the new Doge, not clad
As DOGE, but simply as a senator.

MARINA - I have heard of murderers, who have interred
Their victims; but ne'er heard, until this hour,
Of so much splendour in hypocrisy
O'er those they slew. I've heard of widows' tears—
Alas! I have shed some—always thanks to you!
I've heard of heirs in sables—you have left none
To the deceased, so you would act the part
Of such. Well, sirs, your will be done! as one day,
I trust, Heaven's will be done too!

CHIEF OF THE TEN - Know you, Lady,
To whom ye speak, and perils of such speech?

MARINA - I know the former better than yourselves;

The latter—like yourselves; and can face both.
Wish you more funerals?

BARBARIGO - Heed not her rash words;
Her circumstances must excuse her bearing.

CHIEF OF THE TEN - We will not note them down.

BARBARIGO - (turning to LOREDANO, who is writing upon his tablets).
What art thou writing,
With such an earnest brow, upon thy tablets?

LOREDANO - (pointing to the Doge's body). That he has paid me!

CHIEF OF THE TEN - What debt did he owe you?

LOREDANO - A long and just one; Nature's debt and mine.

[Curtain falls

Lord Byron – A Short Biography

Byron, one of England's greatest poets, endured a quite difficult background. His father, Captain
John "Mad Jack" Byron had married his second wife, the former Catherine Gordon, a descendant of
Cardinal Beaton and heiress of the Gight estate in Aberdeenshire, Scotland for the same reason that
he married his first: her money. Byron's mother-to-be had to sell her land and title to pay her new
husband's debts and within two years the large estate of £23,500, had been squandered, leaving her
with an annual income in trust of £150. In a move to avoid his creditors, Catherine accompanied her
husband to France in 1786, but returned to England at the end of 1787 in order to give birth to her
son on English soil.

George Gordon Byron was born on January 22nd 1788, in lodgings, at Holles Street in London
although there is a conflicting account of him having been born in Dover.

He was christened, at St Marylebone Parish Church, George Gordon Byron, after his maternal
grandfather, George Gordon of Gight, a descendant of James I of Scotland, who, in 1779, had
committed suicide.

In 1790 Catherine moved back to Aberdeenshire and it was here that Byron spent his childhood. His
father joined them in their lodgings in Queen Street, but the couple quickly separated. Catherine
was prone to mood swings and melancholy. Her husband continued to borrow money from her and
she fell deeper into debt. It was one of these "loans" that allowed him to travel to Valenciennes,
France, where he died in 1791.

When Byron's great-uncle, the "wicked" Lord Byron, died on 21 May 1798, the 10-year-old boy
became the 6th Baron Byron of Rochdale and inherited the ancestral home, Newstead Abbey, in
Nottinghamshire. However the Abbey was in a state of disrepair and it was leased to Lord Grey de
Ruthyn, and others for several years.

Catherine's parenting swung between either spoiling or indulging her son to stubbornly refusing every plea. Her drinking disgusted him, and he mocked her short and corpulent frame. She did retaliate and, in a fit of temper, once called him as "a lame brat", on account of his club-foot, an issue on which we was very sensitive. He referred to himself as "le diable boiteux" ("the limping devil").

Byron early education was taken at Aberdeen Grammar School, and in August 1799 he entered the school of Dr. William Glennie, in Dulwich. He was encouraged to exercise in moderation but could not restrain himself from "violent" bouts in an attempt to overcompensate for his deformed foot. His mother interfered, often withdrawing him from school, and resulting in him lacking discipline and neglecting his classical studies.

In 1801 he was sent to Harrow, where he remained until July 1805. Byron was an excellent orator but undistinguished student and an unskilled cricketer but strangely he did represent the school in the very first Eton v Harrow cricket match at Lord's in 1805.

Byron, always prone to over-indulge, fell in love with Mary Chaworth, whom he met while at school, and thence refused to return to Harrow in September 1803. His mother wrote, "He has no indisposition that I know of but love, desperate love, the worst of all maladies in my opinion. In short, the boy is distractedly in love with Miss Chaworth."

He did finally return in January 1804, and described his friends there; "My school friendships were with me passions for I was always violent." His nostalgic poems about his Harrow friendships, in his book Childish Recollections, published in 1806, talk of a "consciousness of sexual differences that may in the end make England untenable to him".

The following autumn he attended Trinity College, Cambridge, where he met and formed a close bond with John Edleston. On his "protégé" Byron wrote, "He has been my almost constant associate since October, 1805, when I entered Trinity College. His voice first attracted my attention, his countenance fixed it, and his manners attached me to him forever." In his memory Byron composed Thyrza, a series of elegies. In later years Byron described the affair as "a violent, though pure love and passion". The public were beginning to view homosexuality with increasing distaste and the law now specified such sanctions as public hanging against convicted or even suspected offenders. Though equally Byron may just be using 'pure' out of respect for Edleston's innocence, in contrast to the more sexually overt relations experienced at Harrow School. Byron is now thought of as bi-sexual though more fulfilled, on all levels, by women.

While not at school or college, Byron lived with his mother in Southwell, Nottinghamshire. While there, he cultivated friendships with Elizabeth Pigot and her brother, John, with whom he staged two plays for the entertainment of the local community. During this time, with the help of Elizabeth, who copied his rough drafts, he wrote his first volumes of poetry, Fugitive Pieces, which included poems written when Byron was only 14. However, it was promptly recalled and burned on the advice of his friend, the Reverend J. T. Becher, on account of its more amorous verses, particularly the poem To Mary.

Hours of Idleness, which collected many of the previous poems, along with recent compositions, was the culminating book. The savage, anonymous criticism this received in the Edinburgh Review prompted his first major satire, English Bards and Scotch Reviewers in 1809. This was put into the hands of his relative, R. C. Dallas, requesting him to "...get it published without his name". Although published anonymously Byron was generally known to be the author. The work so upset some of his critics they challenged Byron to a duel. Of course, over time, it became a mark of renown to be the target of Byron's pen.

Byron first took his seat in the House of Lords March 13th, 1809. He was a strong advocate of social reform, and one of the few Parliamentary defenders of the Luddites: specifically, he was against a death penalty for Luddite "frame breakers" in Nottinghamshire, who destroyed the textile machines that were putting them out of work. His first speech before the Lords, on February 27th, 1812, sarcastically referenced the "benefits" of automation, which he saw as producing inferior material as well as putting people out of work, and concluded the proposed law was only missing two things to be effective: "Twelve Butchers for a Jury and a Jeffries for a Judge!"

Two months later, Byron made another impassioned speech before the House in support of Catholic emancipation. He expressed opposition to the established religion because it was unfair to people who practiced other faiths.

Out of this period would follow several overtly political poems; Song for the Luddites (1816), The Landlords' Interest, Canto XIV of The Age of Bronze, Wellington: The Best of the Cut-Throats (1819) and The Intellectual Eunuch Castlereagh (1818).

Like his father Byron racked up numerous debts. His mother thought he had "reckless disregard for money" and lived in fear of her son's creditors.

Between 1809 to 1811, Byron went on the Grand Tour, then customary for a young nobleman. The Napoleonic Wars meant most of Europe had to be avoided, and he instead ventured south to the Mediterranean.

There is some correspondence among his circle of Cambridge friends that suggests that another motive was the hope of homosexual experience, and other theories saying that he was worried about a possible dalliance with a married woman, Mary Chaworth, his former love.

But other possibilities exist. Byron had read much about the Ottoman and Persian lands as a child, was attracted to Islam (especially Sufi mysticism), and later wrote, "With these countries, and events connected with them, all my really poetical feelings begin and end."

Byron began his trip in Portugal from where he wrote a letter to his friend Mr. Hodgson in which he describes his mastery of the Portuguese language, consisting mainly of swearing and insults. Byron particularly enjoyed his stay in Sintra that is described in Childe Harold's Pilgrimage as "glorious Eden". From Lisbon he travelled overland to Seville, Jerez de la Frontera, Cádiz, Gibraltar and from there by sea on to Malta and Greece.

While in Athens, Byron met 14-year-old Nicolò Giraud, who became quite close and taught him Italian. Byron sent Giraud to school at a monastery in Malta and in his will, though later taken out, bequeathed him a sizeable sum.

Byron then moved on to Smyrna, and then Constantinople on board HMS Salsette. While HMS Salsette was anchored awaiting Ottoman permission to dock at the city, on May 3rd, 1810 Byron and Lieutenant Ekenhead, of Salsette 's Marines, swam the Hellespont. Byron commemorated this feat in the second canto of Don Juan.

When he sailed back to England in April 1811, he travelled, for a time, aboard the transport ship Hydra, which had on board the last large shipments of Lord Elgin's marbles, a piece of vandalism that Byron had longed railed against. The last leg of his voyage home was from Malta in aboard HMS Volage. He arrived at Sheerness, Kent, on July 14th. He was home after two years away.

On August 2nd, his mother died. "I had but one friend in the world," he exclaimed, "and she is gone."

The following year, 1812, Byron became a sensation with the publication, via his literary agent and family relative R. C. Dallas, of the first two cantos of 'Childe Harold's Pilgrimage'. He rapidly became the most brilliant star in the dazzling world of Regency London, sought after at every society venue, elected to several exclusive clubs, and frequented the most fashionable London drawing-rooms. His own words recall; "I awoke one morning and found myself famous". The Edinburgh Review allowed that Byron had "improved marvellously since his last appearance at our tribunal." He followed up his success with the poem's last two cantos, as well as four equally celebrated "Oriental Tales": The Giaour, The Bride of Abydos, The Corsair and Lara.

His affair with Lady Caroline Lamb (who called him "mad, bad and dangerous to know"), as well as other women and the constant pressure of debt, caused him to seek a suitable marriage i.e. marry wealth. One choice was Annabella Milbanke. But in 1813 he met again, after four years, his half-sister, Augusta Leigh. Rumours of incest constantly surrounded the pair; Augusta, who was married, gave birth on April 15th, 1814 to her third daughter, Elizabeth Medora Leigh, and Byron is suspected to be the father.

To escape from debts and rumours he now sought, in earnest, to marry Annabella, (said to be the likely heiress of a rich uncle). They married on January 2nd, 1815, and their daughter, Ada, was born in December of that year. However Byron's continuing obsession with Augusta and dalliances with others made their marriage a misery.

Annabella thought Byron insane and she left him, taking Ada, in January 1816 and began proceedings for a legal separation. For Byron the scandal of the separation, the continuing rumours about Augusta, and ever-increasing debts were to now force him to leave England.

He passed through Belgium and along the river Rhine and by the summer was settled at the Villa Diodati by Lake Geneva, Switzerland, with his personal physician, the young, brilliant, and handsome John William Polidori. There Byron befriended the poet Percy Bysshe Shelley, and his future wife Mary Godwin. He was also joined by Mary's stepsister, Claire Clairmont, with whom, almost inevitably, he had had an affair with in London.

Kept indoors at the Villa Diodati by the incessant rain during three days in June, the five turned to writing. Mary Shelley produced what would become Frankenstein, or The Modern Prometheus, and Polidori was inspired by a fragmentary story of Byron's, Fragment of a Novel, to produce The Vampyre, the progenitor of the romantic vampire genre.

Byron's story fragment was published as a postscript to Mazeppa; he also now wrote the third canto of Childe Harold.

Byron wintered in Venice, pausing his travels when he fell in love with Marianna Segati, in whose Venice house he was lodging, but who was soon replaced by 22-year-old Margarita Cogni; both women were married. Cogni, who could not read or write, left her husband to move into Byron's Venice house. Their fighting often caused Byron to spend nights in his gondola; when he asked her to leave the house, she threw herself into the Venetian canal.

In a visit to San Lazzaro degli Armeni in Venice, he began to immerse himself in Armenian culture. He learned the Armenian language, and attended many seminars about language and history. He co-authored English Grammar and Armenian in 1817, and Armenian Grammar and English in 1819, where he included quotations from classical and modern Armenian and later, in 1821, participated in the compilation of the English Armenian dictionary, and in the preface he mapped out the relationship of the Armenians with, and the oppression of, the Turkish "pashas" and the Persian satraps, and their struggle for liberation.

In 1817 after a visit to Rome and back in Venice, he wrote the fourth canto of Childe Harold and sold his ancestral home, Newstead Abbey, as well as publishing Manfred; A Dramatic Poem and , Cain; A Mystery.

Byron wrote the first five cantos of his renowned Don Juan between 1818 and 1820. And besides work and adventure there was always love. Women, of course, were always in evidence and the young Countess Teresa Guiccioli found her first love in Byron, who in turn asked her to elope with him. They lived in Ravenna between 1819 and 1821 where he continued Don Juan and also wrote the Ravenna Diary, My Dictionary and Recollections.

It was here that he now received visits from Percy Bysshe Shelley and Thomas Moore.

Of Byron's lifestyle in Ravenna Shelley informs us that; "Lord Byron gets up at two. I get up, quite contrary to my usual custom ... at 12. After breakfast we sit talking till six. From six to eight we gallop through the pine forest which divide Ravenna from the sea; we then come home and dine, and sit up gossiping till six in the morning. I don't suppose this will kill me in a week or fortnight, but I shall not try it longer. Lord B.'s establishment consists, besides servants, of ten horses, eight enormous dogs, three monkeys, five cats, an eagle, a crow, and a falcon; and all these, except the horses, walk about the house, which every now and then resounds with their unarbitrated quarrels, as if they were the masters of it... . [P.S.] I find that my enumeration of the animals in this Circean Palace was defective .... I have just met on the grand staircase five peacocks, two guinea hens, and an Egyptian crane. I wonder who all these animals were before they were changed into these shapes."

From 1821 to 1822, he finished Cantos 6–12 of Don Juan at Pisa, and in the same year he joined with Leigh Hunt and Percy Bysshe Shelley in starting a short-lived newspaper, The Liberal, in the first number of which appeared The Vision of Judgment.

For the first time since his arrival in Italy, Byron found himself tempted to give dinner parties; his guests included the Shelleys, Edward Ellerker Williams, Thomas Medwin, John Taaffe and Edward John Trelawney; and "never", as Shelley said, "did he display himself to more advantage than on these occasions; being at once polite and cordial, full of social hilarity and the most perfect good humour; never diverging into ungraceful merriment, and yet keeping up the spirit of liveliness throughout the evening."

Byron's mother-in-law Judith Noel, the Hon. Lady Milbanke, died in 1822. Her will required that he change his surname to "Noel" in order for him to inherit half of her estate. He obtained a Royal Warrant allowing him to "take and use the surname of Noel only". The Royal Warrant also allowed him to "subscribe the said surname of Noel before all titles of honour", and from that point he signed himself "Noel Byron" (the usual signature of a peer being merely the peerage, in this case simply "Byron").

The Shelley's and Williams had rented a house on the coast and had a schooner built. Byron decided that he too should have his own yacht, and engaged Trelawny's friend, Captain Daniel Roberts, to design and construct the boat. It was named the Bolivar.

On July 8th, 1822 Shelley drowned in a boating accident. Byron attended the funeral. Shelley was cremated on the beach at Viareggio where his body had washed up. His ashes were later interred in Rome in the cemetery in Rome where lay already his son William and John Keats.

Byron was living in Genoa when, in 1823, while growing bored, he accepted a call for his help from representatives of the movement for Greek independence from the Ottoman Empire. With the assistance of his banker and Captain Daniel Roberts, Byron chartered the Brig Hercules to take him to Greece. On 16 July, Byron left Genoa arriving at Kefalonia in the Ionian Islands on August 4th.

Byron had spent £4,000 of his own money to refit the Greek fleet and sailed for Missolonghi in western Greece, arriving on December 29th, to join Alexandros Mavrokordatos, a Greek politician with military power. When the famous Danish sculptor Bertel Thorvaldsen heard about Byron's heroics in Greece, he voluntarily re-sculpted his earlier bust of Byron in Greek marble.

Mavrokordatos and Byron planned to attack the Turkish-held fortress of Lepanto, at the mouth of the Gulf of Corinth. Byron employed a fire-master to prepare artillery and took part of the rebel army under his own command, despite his lack of military experience. Before the expedition could sail, on February 15th, 1824, he fell ill, and the usual remedy of bloodletting weakened him further. He made a partial recovery, but in early April he caught a violent cold which further therapeutic bleeding, insisted on by his doctors, aggravated. He developed a violent fever, and died in Missolonghi on April 19th.

Alfred, Lord Tennyson would later recall the shocked reaction in Britain when word was received of Byron's death. The Greeks mourned Lord Byron deeply, and he became a hero. The Greek form of "Byron", continues in popularity as a name in Greece, and a town near Athens is called Vyronas in his honour.

Byron's body was embalmed, but the Greeks wanted their hero to stay with them. Some say his heart was removed to remain in Missolonghi. His body was returned to England (despite his dying wishes that it should not) for burial in Westminster Abbey, but the Abbey refused to accept it on the grounds of "questionable morality".

Huge crowds viewed his body as he lay in state for two days in London before being buried at the Church of St. Mary Magdalene in Hucknall, Nottinghamshire. A marble slab given by the King of Greece is laid directly above Byron's grave.

Byron's friends had raised the sum of £1,000 to commission a statue of the writer by the sculptor Thorvaldsen. However for a decade after the statue was completed, in 1834, most British institutions had refused to accept it, among them the British Museum, St. Paul's Cathedral, Westminster Abbey and the National Gallery, and it remained in storage. Finally Trinity College, Cambridge, placed the statue in its library.

Finally, in 1969, a145 years after Byron's death, a memorial to him was placed in Westminster Abbey. It had been pointedly noted by the New York Times that "People are beginning to ask whether this ignoring of Byron is not a thing of which England should be ashamed ... a bust or a tablet might be put in the Poets' Corner and England be relieved of ingratitude toward one of her really great sons." At last Byron was where he should be.

Lord Byron – A Concise Bibliography

The Major Works
Hours of Idleness (1807)
English Bards and Scotch Reviewers (1809)
Childe Harold's Pilgrimage, Cantos I & II (1812)
The Giaour (1813)
The Bride of Abydos (1813)
The Corsair (1814)
Lara, A Tale (1814)
Hebrew Melodies (1815)
The Siege of Corinth (1816)
Parisina (1816)
The Prisoner of Chillon (1816)
The Dream (1816)
Prometheus (1816)
Darkness (1816)
Manfred (1817)
The Lament of Tasso (1817)
Beppo (1818)
Childe Harold's Pilgrimage (1818)
Don Juan (1819–1824; incomplete on Byron's death in 1824)
Mazeppa (1819)
The Prophecy of Dante (1819)
Marino Faliero (1820)
Sardanapalus (1821)
The Two Foscari (1821)
Cain (1821)
The Vision of Judgment (1821)
Heaven and Earth (1821)
Werner (1822)
The Age of Bronze (1823)
The Island (1823)
The Deformed Transformed (1824)

Index of Titles (This is an abbreviated, not a complete, list of his poems).

A
Address, spoken at the Opening of Drury-Lane Theatre, Saturday, October 10, 1812
The Adieu
Adieu to the Muse (same as "Farewell to the Muse")
Address intended to be recited at the Caledonian Meeting
Adrian's Address to his Soul when Dying
The Age of Bronze (a transcription project)
"All is Vanity, Saith the Preacher"
And Thou Art Dead, as Young and Fair
And Wilt Thou Weep When I am Low?

Another Simple Ballat
Answer to —'s Professions of Affection
Answer to a Beautiful Poem
Answer to Some Elegant Verses Sent by a Friend to the Author, & etc.
Answer to the Foregoing, Addressed to Miss —
Aristomenes
Away, Away, Ye Notes of Woe!

B

Ballad
Beppo, a Venetian Story
The Blues, a Literary Eclogue
Bowles and Campbell
The Bride of Abydos, a Turkish Tale (A transcription project)
Bright Be the Place of Thy Soul! (see "Stanzas for Music")
By the Rivers of Babylon We Sat Down and Wept
"By the Waters of Babylon"

C

Cain, a Mystery (A transcription project)
The Chain I gave (same as "From the Turkish")
The Charity Ball
Childe Harold's Good Night (from Childe Harold's Pilgrimage, Canto I.)
Childe Harold's Pilgrimage
Childish Recollections
Churchill's Grave
The Conquest
The Cornelian
The Corsair: A Tale
The Curse of Minerva

D

Damætas
Darkness
The Death of Calmar and Orla
The Deformed Transformed, a drama (A transcription project)
The Destruction of Sennacherib
The Devil's Drive
Don Juan
A Dream (same as "Darkness")
The Dream
The Duel

E

E Nihilo Nihil; or, An Epigram Bewitched
Egotism. A Letter to J. T. Becher
Elegiac Stanzas on the Death of Sir Peter Parker, Bart.
Elegy
Elegy on Newstead Abbey
Elegy on the Death of Sir Peter Parker (same "Elegiac Stanzas on the Death of Sir Peter Parker, Bart.")
Endorsement to the Deed of Separation, in the April of 1816

English Bards, and Scotch Reviewers, a Satire
Epigram (If for Silver, or for Gold)
Epigram (In Digging up your Bones, Tom Paine)
Epigram (It Seems That the Braziers Propose Soon to Pass)
Epigram (The world is a bundle of hay)
Epigram on an Old Lady Who Had Some Curious Notions Respecting the Soul
Epigrams (Oh, Castlereagh! Thou Art a Patriot Now)
Epilogue
The Episode of Nisus and Euryalus (A Paraphrase from the Æneid, Lib. 9.)
Epistle from Mr. Murray to Dr. Polidori
Epistle to a Friend
Epistle to Augusta
Epistle to Mr. Murray
Epitaph
Epitaph for Joseph Blacket, Late Poet and Shoemaker
Epitaph for William Pitt
Epitaph on a Beloved Friend
Epitaph on a Friend (same as "Epitaph on a Beloved Friend")
Epitaph on John Adams, of Southwell
Epitaph to a Dog
Euthanasia

F

Fame, Wisdom, Love, and Power Were Mine (same as "All is Vanity, saith the Preacher")
Fare Thee Well
Farewell (same as "Farewell! if Ever Fondest Prayer")
Farewell Petition to J. C. H., Esqre.
Farewell to Malta
Farewell to the Muse
Fill the Goblet Again
The First Kiss of Love
A Fragment (Could I Remount the River of My Years)
Fragment (Hills of Annesley, Bleak and Barren)
A Fragment (When, to Their Airy Hall, my Fathers' Voice)
Fragment from the "Monk of Athos"
Fragment of a Translation from the 9th Book of Virgil's Æneid (compare "The Episode of Nisus and Euryalus")
Fragment of an Epistle to Thomas Moore
Fragments of School Exercises: From the "Prometheus Vinctus" of Æschylus
Francesca of Rimini
Francisca
From Anacreon Ode 3. ('Twas Now the Hour When Night Had Driven)
From Job (same as "A Spirit Passed Before Me")
From the French (Ægle, Beauty and Poet, Has Two Little Crimes)
From the French (Must Thou Go, my Glorious Chief)
From the Last Hill That Looks on Thy Once Holy Dome (same as "On the Day of the Destruction of Jerusalem by Titus")
From the Portuguese
From the Turkish (same as "The Chain I Gave")

G

G. G. B. to E. P. (same as "To M. S. G.") (When I Dream That You Love Me, you'll surely Forgive)
The Giaour
The Girl of Cadiz
Granta. A Medley

H

The Harp the Monarch Minstrel Swept
Heaven and Earth, a Mystery (A transcription project)
Hebrew Melodies
Herod's Lament for Mariamne
Hints from Horace (A transcription project)
Hours of Idleness

I

I Speak Not, I Trace Not, I Breathe Not Thy Name (see "Stanzas for Music")
I Saw Thee Weep
I Would I Were a Careless Child
Ich Dien
If Sometimes in the Haunts of Men
If That High World
Imitated from Catullus
Imitation of Tibullus
Impromptu
Impromptu, in Reply to a Friend
In the Valley of Waters (same as "By the Waters of Babylon")
Inscription on the Monument of a Newfoundland Dog
The Island, or Christian and His Comrades
The Irish Avatar
It is the Hour (compare with first stanza of Parisina)

J

Jeptha's Daughter
John Keats
Journal in Cephalonia
Julian [a Fragment]

K

L

La Revanche
Lachin y Gair
L'Amitié est L'Amour sans Ailes
The Lament of Tasso
Lara: A Tale
Last Words on Greece
Lines Addressed by Lord Byron to Mr. Hobhouse on his Election for Westminster
Lines Addressed to a Young Lady
Lines Addressed to the Rev. J. T. Becher
Lines Inscribed Upon a Cup Formed From a Skull
Lines in the Travellers' Book at Orchomenus
Lines on Hearing That Lady Byron Was Ill

Lines on Sir Peter Parker (same as "Elegiac Stanzas on the Death of Sir Peter Parker, Bart.")
Lines to a Lady Weeping (same as "To a Lady Weeping")
Lines to Mr. Hodgson
Lines Written Beneath a Picture
Lines Written Beneath an Elm in the Churchyard of Harrow
Lines Written in an Album, At Malta
Lines Written in "Letters of an Italian Nun and an English Gentleman
Lines Written on a Blank Leaf of The Pleasures of Memory
Lord Byron's Verses on Sam Rogers
Love and Death
Love and Gold
A Love Song. To — (same as "Remind me not, Remind me not")
Love's Last Adieu
Lucietta. A Fragment

M

Maid of Athens, Ere We Part
Manfred, a Dramatic Poem
Marino Faliero, Doge of Venice, an Historical Tragedy (1821) (A transcription project)
Martial, Lib. I. Epig. I.
Mazeppa
Monody on the Death of the Right Hon. R. B. Sheridan
The Morgante Maggiore (A transcription project)
My Boy Hobbie O
My Epitaph
My Soul is Dark

N

Napoleon's Farewell
Napoleon's Snuff-box
The New Vicar of Bray
Newstead Abbey

O

An Occasional Prologue
Ode from the French
Ode on Venice
Ode to a Lady Whose Lover was Killed by a Ball, Which at the Same Time Shivered a Portrait Next His Heart
Ode to Napoleon Buonaparte
An Ode to the Framers of the Frame Bill
Oh! Snatched Away in Beauty's Bloom
Oh! Weep for Those
On a Change of Masters at a Great Public School
On a Cornelian Heart Which Was Broken
On a Distant View of the Village and School of Harrow on the Hill, 1806
On a Royal Visit to the Vaults (Windsor Poetics)
On Being Asked What Was the "Origin of Love"
On Finding a Fan
On Jordan's Banks
On Leaving Newstead Abbey

On Lord Thurlow's Poems
On Moore's Last Operatic Farce, or Farcical Opera
On My Thirty-third Birthday
On My Wedding-Day
On Napoleon's Escape from Elba
On Parting
On Revisiting Harrow
On Sam Rogers (same as "Lord Byron's Verses on Sam Rogers")
On the Birth of John William Rizzo Hoppner
On the Bust of Helen by Canova
On the Day of the Destruction of Jerusalem by Titus
On the Death of — Thyrza (same as "To Thyrza")
On the Death of a Young Lady
On the Death of Mr. Fox
On the Death of the Duke of Dorset
On the Eyes of Miss A— H—
On the Quotation
On the Star of "the Legion of Honour"
On this Day I complete my Thirty-sixth Year
One Struggle More, and I Am Free
Oscar of Alva
Ossian's Address to the Sun in "Carthon"

P

Parenthetical Address
Parisina
Pignus Amoris
The Prayer of Nature
The Prisoner of Chillon
The Prophecy of Dante, a Poem

Q

Quem Deus Vult Perdere Prius Dementat
Queries to Casuists

R

R. C. Dallas
Remember Him, whom Passion's Power
Remember Thee! Remember thee!
Remembrance
Remind Me Not, Remind Me Not
Reply to Some Verses of J. M. B. Pigot, Esq., on the Cruelty of his Mistress

S

Sardanapalus, a Tragedy (A transcription project)
Saul
She Walks in Beauty
The Siege of Corinth
A Sketch From Life
So We'll Go No More A-Roving
Soliloquy of a Bard in the Country

Sonetto di Vittorelli
Song (Breeze of the Night in Gentler Sighs)
Song (Fill the Goblet Again! For I Never Before)
Song (Maid of Athens, Ere We Part) (same as "Maid of Athens, Ere We Part")
Song (Thou Art Not False, But Thou Art fickle) same as "Thou Art Not False, But Thou Art Fickle")
Song (When I Roved a Young Highlander) (same as "When I Roved a Young Highlander")
Song For the Luddites
Song of Saul Before His Last Battle
Song To the Suliotes
Sonnet On Chillon
Sonnet on the Nuptials of the Marquis Antonio Cavalli with the Countess Clelia Rasponi of Ravenna
Sonnet, to Genevra (Thine eyes' Blue Tenderness, Thy Long Fair Hair)
Sonnet, to Generva (Thy Cheek is Pale with Thought, but Not From Woe). aka "Sonnet, to the Same"
Sonnet to Lake Leman
Sonnet to the Prince Regent
The Spell is Broke, the Charm is Flown!
A Spirit Passed Before Me
Stanzas (And Thou Art Dead, as Young and Fair)
Stanzas (And Wilt Thou Weep When I am Low?) (same as "And Wilt Thou Weep When I Am Low?")
Stanzas (Away, Away, Ye Notes of Woe)
Stanzas (Chill and Mirk is the Nightly Blast) (same as "Stanzas Composed During a Thunderstorm")
Stanzas (Could Love For Ever)
Stanzas (I Would I Were a Careless Child) (same as "I Would I Were a Careless Child")
Stanzas (If Sometimes in the Haunts of Men)
Stanzas (One Struggle More, and I Am Free)
Stanzas (Remember Him, Whom Passion's Power)
Stanzas (Thou Art Not False, but Thou Art Fickle)
Stanzas (Through Cloudless Skies, in Silvery Sheen) (same as "Stanzas Written in Passing the Ambracian Gulf")
Stanzas (When a Man Hath No Freedom to Fight For at Home)
Stanzas Composed During a Thunderstorm
Stanzas For Music (Bright Be the Place of Thy Soul!)
Stanzas For Music (I Speak Not, I Trace Not, I Breathe Not Thy Name)
Stanzas For Music (There Be None of Beauty's Daughters)
Stanzas For Music (There's Not a Joy the World Can Give Like That it Takes Away)
Stanzas For Music (They Say That Hope is Happiness)
Stanzas To — (same as "Stanzas to Augusta": Though the Day of My Destiny's Over)
Stanzas To a Hindoo Air
Stanzas To a Lady, on Leaving England
Stanzas To a Lady, with the Poems of Camoëns
Stanzas To Augusta (When all around grew drear and dark)
Stanzas To Augusta (Though the day of my Destiny's over)
Stanzas To Jessy
Stanzas To the Po
Stanzas To the Same (same as "There was a Time, I need not name")
Stanzas Written in Passing the Ambracian Gulf
Stanzas Written on the Road Between Florence and Pisa
Substitute For an Epitaph
Sun of the Sleepless!
Sympathetic Address to a Young Lady (same as "Lines to a Lady Weeping")

T

The Tear

There Be None of Beauty's Daughters (see "Stanzas for Music")

There Was a Time, I Need Not Name

There's Not a Joy the World Can Give Like That it Takes Away (see "Stanzas for Music")

They say that Hope is Happiness (see "Stanzas for Music")

Thou Art Not False, but Thou Art Fickle

Thou Whose Spell Can Raise the Dead (same as "Saul")

Thoughts Suggested by a College Examination

Thy Days are Done

To — (But Once I Dared to Lift My Eyes)

To — (Oh! Well I Know Your Subtle Sex)

To A— (same as "To M—")

To a Beautiful Quaker

To a Knot of Ungenerous Critics

To a Lady (Oh! Had My Fate Been Join'd with Thine)

To a Lady (This Band, Which Bound Thy yellow Hair)

To a Lady (When Man, Expell'd from Eden's Bowers)

To a Lady Weeping (same as "Lines To a Lady Weeping")

To a Lady who Presented to the Author a Lock of Hair Braided with His Own, and Appointed a Night in December to Meet Him in the Garden

To a Vain Lady

To a Youthful Friend

To an Oak at Newstead

To Anne (Oh, Anne, Your Offences to Me Have Been Grievous)

To Anne (Oh Say Not, Sweet Anne, That the Fates Have Decreed)

To Belshazzar

To Caroline (Oh! When Shall the Grave Hide For Ever My Sorrow?)

To Caroline (Think'st thou I saw thy beauteous eyes)

To Caroline (When I Hear you Express an Affection so Warm)

To Caroline (You Say You Love, and Yet Your Eye)

To D—

To Dives. A Fragment

To E—

To Edward Noel Long, Esq.

To Eliza

To Emma

To E. N. L. Esq. (same as "To Edward Noel Long, Esq.")

To Florence

To George Anson Byron (?)

To George, Earl Delawarr

To Harriet

To Ianthe (The "Origin of Love!"—Ah, why) (same as "On Being Asked What Was the 'Origin of Love'")

To Ianthe (from Canto I of Childe Harold's Pilgrimage) (Not in Those Climes Where I Have Late Been Straying)

To Inez (from Canto I of Childe Harold's Pilgrimage) (Nay, Smile Not at My Sullen Brow)

To Julia (same as "To Lesbia!")

To Lesbia!

To Lord Thurlow

To M—

To Maria — (same as "To Emma")
To Mrs. — (same as "Well! Thou Art Happy")
To Mrs. Musters (same as "Stanzas To a Lady, On Leaving England")
To M. S. G. (When I Dream That You Love Me, You'll Surely Forgive)
To M. S. G. (Whene'er I View Those Lips of Thine)
To Marion
To Mary, on Receiving Her Picture
To Miss E. P. (same as "To Eliza")
To Mr. Murray (For Orford and for Waldegrave)
To Mr. Murray (Strahan, Tonson, Lintot of the Times)
To Mr. Murray (To Hook the Reader, You, John Murray)
To my Son
To Penelope
To Romance
To Samuel Rogers, Esq. (same as "Lines Written On a Blank Leaf of The Pleasures of Memory")
To Sir W. D. (same as "To a Youthful Friend")
To the Author of a Sonnet
To the Countess of Blessington
To the Duke of D— (same as "To the Duke of Dorset")
To the Duke of Dorset
To the Earl of — (same as "To the Earl of Clare")
To the Earl of Clare
To the Honble. Mrs. George Lamb
To the Prince Regent on the Repeal of the Bill of Attainder Against Lord E. Fitzgerald, June, 1819. (same as "Sonnet to the Prince Regent")
To the Rev. J. T. Becher (same as "Lines: Addressed to the Rev. J. T. Becher")
To the Same (same as "And Wilt Thou Weep When I Am Low?")
To the Sighing Strephon
To Thomas Moore (My Boat is on the Shore)
To Thomas Moore (Oh you, Who in all Names Can Tickle the Town)
To Thomas Moore (What Are You Doing Now)
To Thyrza (Without a Stone to Mark the Spot)
To Thyrza (One Struggle More, and I Am Free) (same as "One Struggle More, and I am Free")
To Time
To Woman
Translation from Anacreon Ode 1. (I Wish to Tune My Quivering Lyre)
Translation from Anacreon Ode 5. (Mingle with the Genial Bowl)
Translation from Catullus: Ad Lesbiam
Translation from Catullus: Lugete Veneres Cupidinesque
Translation from Horace
Translation from the "Medea" of Euripides [Ll. 627–660]
Translation from Vittorelli
Translation of a Romaic Love Song
Translation of the Epitaph on Virgil and Tibullus, by Domitius Marsus
Translation of the Famous Greek War Song
Translation of the Nurse's Dole in the Medea of Euripides
Translation of the Romaic Song
The Two Foscari, a Tragedy (A transcription project)

U

V

Venice. A Fragment
Verses Found in a Summer-house at Hales-Owen
Versicles
A Version of Ossian's Address to the Sun
A very Mournful Ballad on the Siege and Conquest of Alhama
Vision of Belshazzar
The Vision of Judgment (A transcription project)
A Volume of Nonsense

W

The Waltz, an Apostrophic Hymn
Warriors and Chiefs! (same as "Song of Saul Before His Last Battle")
We Sate Down and Wept by the Waters of Babel (same as "By the Rivers of Babylon We Sat Down and Wept")
Well! Thou art Happy
Were My Bosom as False as Thou Deem'st It To Be
Werner, or The Inheritance, a Tragedy (A transcription project)
When a Man Hath No Freedom to Fight For at Home (see "Stanzas")
When Coldness Wraps This Suffering Clay
When I Roved a Young Highlander
When We Two Parted
The Wild Gazelle
Windsor Poetics
A Woman's Hair
Written after Swimming from Sestos to Abydos
Written at Athens (same as "The Spell is Broke, the Charm is Flown!")
Written at the Request of a Lady in her Memorandum Book (same as "Lines Written in an Album, At Malta")
Written in an Album (same as "Lines Written in an Album, At Malta")
Written in Mrs. Spencer S.'s— (same as "Lines Written in an Album, At Malta")